Trying to Say What is True:

Encounters with the Living Word

Georgiana,
    I hope you will find these
words to be true and good
news to you! Keeping you in

my prayers.
                    God bless,
                    Matt Rich

Matthew A. Rich

&

Parson's Porch Books

www.parsonsporchbooks.com

Trying to Say What is True: Encounters with the Living Word
ISBN: Softcover 978-1-949888-54-6
Copyright © 2019 by Matthew A. Rich

All scripture quotations, unless otherwise indicated, are taken from the New Revised Standard Version of the Bible, copyright 1989, Division of Christian Education of the National Council of Churches of Christ in the United States of America.

"What Can Separate Us?" was originally published by pres-outlook.org and is reprinted by permission.

Trying to Say What is True

Contents

Part 3 – Called: Flaws and All

Part 4 – Trying to Say What is True

Foreword

What does "good preaching" look like? That question is as old as the gospel itself and generates as many answers as there are preachers who preach! While some form of oral exhortation and teaching has been part of Judeo-Christian worship since its inception, the precise nature of what preaching *is* and *should do* has remained elusive. Scripture tells us that "Jesus came preaching," but beyond what might be regarded as a few sermon fragments and some instructive sayings and stories, he left those of us who wish to carry on his work deprived of any specific guidelines for Christian proclamation. As a result, preachers and listeners alike have been on an eternal quest to identify the most effective sermons.

While a definitive understanding of preaching and its performative power continues to confound us, there are a number of qualities of effective preaching that have come to define contemporary Christian homiletics and on which most preachers would agree. Preaching must be rooted in the biblical text, the story of God's saving work on our behalf, and it must bear witness to the One through whom that work has been accomplished. But it must also reach beyond the ancient words of scripture to touch our lives today in ways that represent the power and promise of Jesus Christ. Good—or what might be called more appropriately "effective"—preaching is, as theologian Mary Catherine Hilkert suggests, "the art of naming grace found in the depths of human experience."[1] It engages what Hilkert calls the "sacramental imagination," a way of discerning the world that "celebrates the mystery of God's presence here and now, summoning creation to a new future."[2]

In this excellent and exemplary collection of sermons, the Reverend Matthew Rich, whom I was blessed to have first as a preaching student at Union Presbyterian Seminary and now as a colleague in ministry, demonstrates the validity of Hilkert's assertions. In these sermons, we find all the immutable qualities of good preaching:

---

[1] Mary Catherine Hilkert, *Naming Grace: Preaching and the Sacramental Imagination* (New York: Continuum, 1997), 44.
[2] Ibid., 46.

faithfulness to the biblical text, theology that is both sound (according to Reformed understanding) and comprehensible, an engaging style of presentation, and a keen awareness of the longings of the listeners as well as the exigencies of the world in which they live. Matt reaches beyond all these essential qualities, however, to tap into the "sacramental imagination," as Hilkert calls it, inviting his listeners to envision a new way of being according to God's economy and to "name grace": the abundant and immanent grace of God that infuses our lives and world. Whether we are journeying with Jesus once again through Holy Week, sitting with the disciples at Jesus' feet as he teaches us who he truly is, trying to grasp the weight of what it means to be called by God, or wrestling with the astonishing truths of our faith, Matt brings us face-to-face with the grace of God in Jesus Christ. This "encounter with the Living Word," as he calls it, is at the heart of every sermon and calls us to faithful response.

Matt's sermons come to us in what is the best of times and the worst of times for preachers. It is the worst of times due to the cultural chaos that consumes us as well as the increasing disregard for—even derision of—Christian faith. Even the very premise of preaching— the act of one person standing up before a group of passive listeners to deliver a monologue prescribing beliefs and behaviors based on ancient texts—seems ludicrous in our technology- and entertainment-driven world. But this is also the *best* of times for preachers, for few moments in human history have been more desperate for a word from beyond our human capacities than ours. As he demonstrates so well in these sermons, Matt Rich humbly yet confidently steps up to speak such a word. It is a word forged in the crucible of life lived among people seeking to be faithful in a perplexing world. For his own understanding of preaching, Matt claims, as he states in his introduction to this volume, a definition that comes from Marilynne Robinson's exquisite novel *Gilead*: "trying to say what is true." Indeed, in his life and ministry as well as in his preaching, Matt strives to say what is true. He names grace, as Hilkert would call it, and he speaks the truth. Not a bad definition of preaching, for, in the end, what is preaching but bearing witness to the Word who came to dwell among us, "full of grace and truth?" And heaven knows we need all the grace and truth we can muster to help us navigate through these challenging days for the church, and we need preachers like Matt Rich to lead us. So read and ponder this good preaching, these sermons that name grace and tell the truth, and be led anew to encounters with the Living Word.

The Rev. Beverly A. Zink-Sawyer, Ph.D.

Professor Emerita of Preaching and Worship
Union Presbyterian Seminary
Richmond, Virginia

Introduction

In the novel *Gilead* by Marilynne Robinson, the protagonist, John Ames, is an aging Congregationalist pastor. Ames married very late in life and has a young son who is just eight years old. Fearing that the end of his life is near and wanting to share some of his life, his thoughts, and his family history with his son, Ames writes an extended letter that he hopes his son will read someday long after Ames himself is dead. In one passage, he reflects upon the sermons he has written:

> My father preached from notes, and I wrote my sermons out word for word. There are boxes of them in the attic, a few recent years of them in stacks in the closet. I've never gone back to them to see if they were worth anything, if I actually said anything. Pretty nearly my whole life's work is in those boxes, which is an amazing thing to reflect on. ... I wrote almost all of it in the deepest love and conviction. Sifting my thoughts and choosing my words. Trying to say what was true.[3]

Yes, sifting thoughts and choosing words. Trying to say what is true. That is one of the better descriptions of the task of preaching that I have ever read. As John Ames discovered it is an odd thing to go back and read even a year's worth of sermons as I have done for this volume. Once again I have been forced to sift thoughts and chose words, to see if they were worth anything. As you begin to read, I hope and I pray that the words in these pages are as close as I can come to saying what is true.

I have divided the sermons into four sections. The first three sections are respectively from Holy Week, the Easter Season, and a summer lectionary series from 1 and 2 Samuel that we titled, "Called: Flaws and All." The final section includes sermons which are more occasional, responding to a particular joy or tragedy, creating

---

[3] Marilynne Robinson, *Gilead* (New York: Farrar, Straus, Giroux, 2004) 18-19.

conversation with a current event or opportunity in the life of the congregation. Together they contain a representative sample of the truth I sought to proclaim.

It is an amazing gift and humbling privilege to climb into the pulpit each Sunday at Reid Memorial Presbyterian Church in Augusta, Georgia. Those who gather to worship appreciate faithful preaching and I seek to honor their trust. All but one of the sermons in this volume were preached at Reid Memorial. All but one of the sermons were preached over the course of 2018.

I am immensely grateful to the members of Reid Memorial for the opportunity to preach, worship, and serve with them. My pastoral colleagues, the Reverend Nadine Ellsworth-Moran and the Reverend Bob Hunt, help make me a better preacher and I hope I share the same gift with them. I also thank the members of First Presbyterian Church, Lumberton, North Carolina; The Presbyterian Church of Lowell; and the Salem-Pageland Presbyterian Church for their patience and care as they nurtured my preaching in the years before God called me to Augusta.

Thank you to David Russell Tullock of Parson's Porch Books who approached me to see if I would be willing to publish a collection of sermons with him and encouraged me to complete the task of preparation and publication.

Thank you also to my friend Jill Duffield, editor and publisher of *The Presbyterian Outlook*, and her predecessor Jack Haberer. Jill and Jack have both been kind to publish my articles and occasional pieces, always encouraging me to write for the greater church. The sermon "What Can Separate Us?" was first published online by *The Presbyterian Outlook* and I thank Jill for permission to include it in this collection.

Twenty years ago at Union Presbyterian Seminary Dr. Beverly Zink-Sawyer taught me to write sermons and read congregations, becoming not just a professor but a mentor and friend. That she would agree to write the foreword to this volume means a great deal to me and I thank her.

I thank my wife Sarah for her love, support and care for me and our family. She makes me a better follower of Jesus, pastor, preacher, and person than I would ever be on my own. Thank you also to our three children, Will, Sam, and Bekah, for their energy, their faith, their joy, and their patience with a father who sees sermon illustrations everywhere. I do seek to honor our pact to always ask their permission before including them in a sermon.

Finally, in addition to hearing me preach on Sundays at Reid Memorial, every Monday morning at 10 AM a dozen or so congregation members gather in the church library for "Monday Musings." With printed copies of Sunday's sermon in hand and bibles open we openly talk about the text and the sermon - both its content and my delivery. Together we seek to truly encounter the living word. My preaching is vastly richer and deeper knowing that we will discuss it on Monday mornings at Musings. They help me say what is true. Monday Musings has become one of the most enjoyable parts of my week. We talked about all of these sermons and more and thus I dedicate this collection to them.

Part 1

Encounters with the Living Word

Why Are You Doing This?

Mark 11:1-11

Palm Sunday

¹When they were approaching Jerusalem, at Bethphage and Bethany, near the Mount of Olives, [Jesus] sent two of his disciples ²and said to them, "Go into the village ahead of you, and immediately as you enter it, you will find tied there a colt that has never been ridden; untie it and bring it. ³If anyone says to you, 'Why are you doing this?' just say this, 'The Lord needs it and will send it back here immediately.'" ⁴They went away and found a colt tied near a door, outside in the street. As they were untying it, ⁵some of the bystanders said to them, "What are you doing, untying the colt?" ⁶They told them what Jesus had said; and they allowed them to take it. ⁷Then they brought the colt to Jesus and threw their cloaks on it; and he sat on it. ⁸Many people spread their cloaks on the road, and others spread leafy branches that they had cut in the fields. ⁹Then those who went ahead and those who followed were shouting,

> *"Hosanna!*
> *Blessed is the one who comes in the name of the Lord!*
> *¹⁰Blessed is the coming kingdom of our ancestor David!*
> *Hosanna in the highest heaven!"*

¹¹Then he entered Jerusalem and went into the temple; and when he had looked around at everything, as it was already late, he went out to Bethany with the twelve.

What do you think the two disciples said when Jesus told them they were on donkey detail? I mean it does not sound like a job for those at the head of the discipleship class. Remember Peter, James, and John – they all get mentioned by name when Jesus takes them up the mountain of transfiguration. Later these same three are named as they get a closer view of Jesus praying in Gethsemane. Last Sunday we heard how some Greeks who want to see Jesus come to two other disciples: Philip and Andrew. Yes, there are some jobs that get your name included in the Bible, but in this text Jesus sends "two of the disciples" to go and borrow a donkey. No names required for this task.

So, yes, these two disciples are given donkey detail. Professor Tom Long describes it like this:

> All of the disciples had been jockeying for advantage, angling for glory, arguing about who was the greatest. So it is deliciously ironic that on this very public and glorious day of Jesus' ministry, a day when he will be welcomed into Jerusalem with joyous hosannas, [these two disciples] find themselves engaged in a most unromantic form of ministry, mucking around a stable, looking suspiciously like horse thieves, and trying to wrestle an untamed and no doubt balky animal toward the olive groves. For this they left their fishing nets?[4]

This is not the job that gets you on the evening news. So why are they doing this?

Yes, why are you doing this? That is the question Jesus himself anticipates will be asked when these two disciples show up in a village and attempt to untie a colt that has never been ridden. Why are you doing this? Jesus knows the question is coming, so he gives them an answer – The Lord needs it.

Yes, the Lord needs it. Hold on to that for a moment.

Because my friends, I wonder if the world is still asking those of us who seek to follow Jesus the same question. Why are you doing this? Yesterday in our nation's capital, in cities across the country, and even here in Augusta there were marches with signs and speakers and journalists from every kind of media to cover it all. Whether you agree with the purpose of the march or not, you have to admit that these parades far surpassed our little procession into the sanctuary this morning, even if we had been able to start on the lawn of the Alan Fuqua Center next door. As Jill Duffield from *The Presbyterian Outlook* wrote this week:

---

[4] Thomas Long, "Palm Sunday – Mark 11:1-11," https://www.christiancentury.org/article/2006-04/rhetorical-excess

We must look an odd sight to those passing by our sanctuaries on Sunday morning as we stand outside with palm branches, some of us dressed in our finest and others in robes, children roaming, youth huddling, all ages gathering to sing and process. Anyone unfamiliar with what week it is (and many will have no idea what week it is on the liturgical calendar) might ask: Why are you doing this? What are you doing? [5]

Yes, we know that here in Augusta the calendar does not say Palm Sunday. Please do not walk out when I tell you this, but the calendar in Augusta says: "7 days remaining before The Masters!" Shouldn't we all be home cleaning our houses instead of walking a quarter of a block carrying palm branches? Why are we doing this?

And once we get inside the sanctuary the questions continue. Because where else do you sing music like this in the course of your normal week? How often does the music we sing and hear in worship ever come through the speakers in your car on the way to work? And yet, every Sunday we sing at least three (and this week four) hymns. Why are we doing this?

Then in the middle of the service this morning I poured water over the head of young Georgia. There are thousands and thousands of children in this community. You can find them everywhere. Some of them have great needs. For example, there are children in the hospital this morning. Others are hungry because they do not have food to eat and the backpack sent home with them from school on Friday is already empty. There are children wondering what will happen when their mother or father wakes up after a night of drinking or drugs.

And then there are also children completely unaware of those challenges. Yes, there are children on soccer fields and baseball fields and in competitions of all kinds this morning. There are children sitting at home playing video games or still asleep. Yes, there are

---

[5] Jill Duffield, "Looking into the Lectionary – Palm/Passion Sunday, March 25, 2018," http://pres-outlook.org/2018/03/march-25-2018-palm-passion-sunday/

children everywhere in this community, but I suspect the only place you will find anyone pouring water over the head of a fully-clothed child is at church. Why are we doing this?

There are many fired up in this community and across this nation, ready to take action. There are letters to be written, visits to be made, Facebook posts to post, tweets to retweet. Why? You pick the issue. There are people trying to take our guns or people who are trying to sell guns to children. There are people destroying the environment or people who think too much regulation hinders development. There are those advocating for a women's right to choose and those advocating for the life of unborn children. There are questions about monuments and how we best remember our history or questions about race and whose lives matter. There are foreign leaders with nuclear weapons and attempts by foreign powers to influence elections and create social chaos; there are data breaches of personal information; there are tweets and press conferences and competing memos. There are new arena sites to find and primary elections to prepare for. Yes, that but scratches the surface of all that is to be done. And this morning, as we gather we ... pray. Yes, the world demands serious answers to serious problems and we ... pray. Why are we doing this?

And don't get me started on the hundreds and thousands of worthwhile, interesting, and passionate voices in the world today, and you have chosen to sit and listen to me. Really? Why are we doing this?

Yes, why are you doing this?

Because the Lord needs us. Remember, that is the answer to the question. Why are you doing this? The Lord needs it. But what about all the work to do and the people who do not understand? The Lord needs us. Again, Tom Long puts it this way:

> It is right at this place ... that Mark imparts some of his best theological wisdom. He begins his Gospel with the exhilarating trumpet call to "prepare the way of the Lord," but he makes it clear, by his description of the disciples'

activity in the rest of his Gospel, that the way to do so is not by becoming a member of the Knights Templar and gallantly defending Christendom, but rather by performing humble and routine tasks. The disciples in Mark get a boat ready for Jesus, find out how much food is on hand for the multitude, secure the room and prepare the table for the Last Supper and, of course, chase down a donkey that the Lord needs to enter Jerusalem. Whatever they may have heard when Jesus beckoned, "Follow me," it has led them into a ministry of handling the gritty details of everyday life. ... We are but donkey fetchers. [And in ways often hidden from our eyes] because we are "preparing the way of the Lord," the routine, often exhausting, seemingly mundane donkey-fetching details of our service are gathered into the great arc of Jesus' redemptive work in the world.[6]

Yes, my friends, at least for this moment the Lord needs us to be right here. Not out saving the world –Jesus has that under control later this week. And soon enough we will be back out there in the world with much work to do. But for this moment, the Lord needs us right here.

Yes, this morning the Lord needs us to not charge to the front, drawing attention to ourselves and our importance. The Lord needs us to pick up a palm branch and follow him, crying out Hosanna – save us now – to the only one who really can.

The Lord needs us to worship in ways that move our hearts and souls, but not necessarily in ways that are all about our preferences and desires. The Lord needs us to sing with those who have sung before as a part of a never ending stream of the faithful.

The Lord needs us to entrust our children to his care, to express with water poured over their heads that they are children of God and we will care for them as our own. The Lord needs us to believe in a future for these children that is secure in the Lord's hands.

---

[6] Long, ibid.

The Lord needs us to remember that all the issues in the world that so occupy our time and attention, all the work that needs to be done, cannot be accomplished on our own. Once again Jill Duffield writes,

> Nothing is off limits to our Lord. That's why we do what we do on Palm Sunday and Maundy Thursday and Good Friday and Easter Sunday and every Sunday afterwards. We make public our loyalty and our love for Jesus Christ, and our commitment to follow the Lord of All, every day, everywhere, anywhere.[7]

Yes, my friends, this most Holy Week begins with fetching a donkey. Along the way we will prepare an upper room for dinner, pray in a garden, flee for our lives, prepare a body for burial, and get up early on the third day. Why are we doing these things? Because the Lord needs us. Yes, the Lord needs us to bear witness that in the big and the small, he is Lord of all. Do not doubt that there is great and necessary work to be done, but for this moment, the Lord knows not just that he needs us, but that we need him.

That's why we do this.

---

[7] Jill Duffield, ibid.

This is My Body
1 Corinthians 11:23-26

Maundy Thursday

23 For I received from the Lord what I also handed on to you, that the Lord Jesus on the night when he was betrayed took a loaf of bread, 24 and when he had given thanks, he broke it and said, "This is my body that is for you. Do this in remembrance of me." 25 In the same way he took the cup also, after supper, saying, "This cup is the new covenant in my blood. Do this, as often as you drink it, in remembrance of me." 26 For as often as you eat this bread and drink the cup, you proclaim the Lord's death until he comes.

She pushed open the door to the diner and slid into a cracked red-vinyl booth by the window. Why was she here? She didn't know.

After the test was positive she almost threw up. Then she threw the box across the bathroom. Hearing the noise her mother knocked softly on the locked door and sweetly asked if she was ok. "Yeah," she lied. "I'm fine." She picked up all the traces of the test, pulled open the door, and declared she was going out for a while. "Ok, honey," her mom almost seemed to sing from the kitchen.

She didn't know how far she had driven, lost in her thoughts and broken dreams. Sure there were teen moms on television, it seemed all the rage in the reality shows, but no one she knew had a baby. What was she going to do? Could she even tell her boyfriend – it's not like they were all that serious. Would her mom ever listen without judging? Could she ever go to church again?

The blinking welcome sign on the diner caught her attention, so she pulled in, got out of the car, came in the door, and slid into the booth. The man behind the counter called out almost distractedly, "Be right there. It's almost ready."

A bell jingled as the door opened again. A young man, maybe late twenties, wearing khaki pants and a V-neck sweater walked in and took a seat on a stool by the counter. He shook his head. Why was he here? He did not know.

An hour ago he had come home from work. He taught science at the local high school. He loved his job, which was a good thing, because he certainly did not do it for the money. Helping the kids discover the wonders of the universe got him up every morning and out the door. His favorite experiment was the ball of static electricity. Whenever things got dull in class, he would pull it out and plug it in. One by one kids came up and rested their hands on the ball. The hair on their arms would begin to stand up, then their heads, like a porcupine! The kids loved to take pictures of that on their cell phones!

It had been a fine day, just like any other, but when he came home he found an unfamiliar truck in the driveway. His wife was standing on the stoop with their two-year old son in her arms waiting on him. She said, "I am leaving you. This town, this boring life, you – I can't take it anymore." He yelled, he cried, he begged, he pleaded all in the three minutes it took her to walk from the stoop, buckle their son into a car seat, get in the truck herself and drive away. As the truck turned the corner at the end of the street he first thought he should follow, but he did not. It must be all his fault, so he got in his car and drove the opposite direction.

He didn't know how long he drove, lost in his thoughts and broken dreams. The blinking welcome sign on the diner caught his attention, so he pulled in, got out of the car, came in the door, and sat down at the counter. He absently picked up a menu as the man behind the counter walked by saying, "Not long now. It's almost ready."

The bell jingled and the door seemed to just hang open for a moment. A woman in a suit, looking at her cell phone, stood in the doorway for a minute just letting the cold air come in. As if suddenly realizing where she was, she entered letting the door close with a bang. She found a seat in a booth at the far side of the diner. Why was she here? She didn't know.

Her phone buzzed. She looked at it and set it on the table. It buzzed again. The pattern continued for several minutes. It had been like this all day, she thought. It is like this every day. Even the weekends. No rest for the weary, but she wasn't supposed to be weary.

It was a little fatigue that sent her to the doctor the first time. She ran her own highly successful business, she didn't have time to go to the doctor, but she did not have time to be sick either. The doctor took some blood, did an x-ray, and said, "Come back next week and I'll let you know if there is anything you need to worry about. Try to get some more sleep and drink less caffeine."

Sure, like that was going to happen.

It was only a day later that the doctor called and said to come in right away. She had meetings all afternoon and then an out of town trip scheduled for the rest of the week. Could it be next week? No, come today, was the reply. So she arranged this and missed that and rescheduled multiple things to carve out an hour. Sitting in the doctor's office it was like she already knew what he was going to say. When the doctor came in, he confirmed her suspicions. Cancer, aggressive.

She didn't know how far she had driven, lost in her thoughts and broken dreams. Her phone kept buzzing and she kept letting calls go to voicemail. How could this happen to her? She was at the top of her game, she was successful! How could she have cancer?

The blinking welcome sign on the diner caught her attention, so she pulled in, got out of the car, came in the door, and slid into the booth. The man behind the counter called out, "Be right with you. It's almost ready."

Another jingle as the door opened to reveal a man holding a hat in his hand. He looked a little bewildered and glanced back and forth around the diner. He then moved into the room, let the door slide shut behind him, and he found a seat in a booth.

He looked down at the table in front of him. He smiled as a memory washed over of a trip they had taken together just after they had

25

gotten married. They didn't have any money so they brought his old army tent along to camp. It was glorious and rustic and perfect … until the rain came. The tent leaked. And it rained and it rained and it rained and it rained! And the leak turned to a drizzle which turned to a downpour. They gathered as much as they could and ran for the car. Soaking wet, they drove until he saw an old diner and pulled in. Still drenched they sat at a table just like this one and talked and drank coffee for hours. It was glorious!

He raised his eyes and opened his mouth to tell her about the memory. He knew that she would smile and even laugh. But she wasn't there. He shuddered as he remembered three days ago standing in the cemetery as they shoveled dirt upon her casket. She never saw the driver swerve into her lane. In an instant, she was gone.

The kids and their families all went home this morning. The house was so quiet he thought he would go for a drive. He didn't know how long he drove, lost in his thoughts and broken dreams. The blinking welcome sign on the diner caught his attention, so he pulled in, got out of the car, came in the door, and sat down. He heard a voice say, "Wonderful. It's time. We're all here."

The man behind the counter smiled at his guests. Their eyes all turned and rested in his eyes as he began to speak with a calm and clear voice. "Welcome to my dinner. I am glad that you all came. I have been waiting for you and preparing for you all day. You may have come to my table often or it may have been a long time since I have met you here, but you are welcome, just like the blinking sign that drew you here said. There is a place for you."

The man lifted a piece of bread with his hands and continued, "So often we talk about my body as bread, and that is true. Bread is a marvelous image for my body. And yet, my friend Paul had it right when he talked about the church as my body too."

The man paused and broke the bread in two. "This is my body, broken for you. Could that be not just the bread on the table, but my body that gathers at the table? This is my body, you are my body.

And you are broken and you are welcomed and you are loved. The only people who have a hard time finding this place are those who refuse to think they are broken. Those who are convinced they can do it all on their own. Those who have no need of a savior. But you, on this day, have gathered here at this table. This is my body, you are my body."

"So I give you a new commandment. Love one another. Just as I have loved you, you also should love one another. By your love for one another, others will see and know that you follow me. By your love, you will welcome to this table others who are broken. By your love the world will know that seats of honor are not for the proud and the self-reliant, but are reserved for the broken."

Then He vanished from their sight. The pregnant teenager, the man with a failed marriage, the busy woman with cancer, the new widower, looked at each other and smiled. It would be ok. They knew that it would be hard and painful and sometimes the way would be dark, but all would be well.

The welcome sign blinked again, this time catching your eye. Those at the table begin to grasp hands and one of them reaches out to you.

This is God's Son
Mark 15:33-41

Good Friday

33 When it was noon, darkness came over the whole land until three in the afternoon. 34 At three o'clock Jesus cried out with a loud voice, "Eloi, Eloi, lema sabachthani?" which means, "My God, my God, why have you forsaken me?" 35 When some of the bystanders heard it, they said, "Listen, he is calling for Elijah." 36 And someone ran, filled a sponge with sour wine, put it on a stick, and gave it to him to drink, saying, "Wait, let us see whether Elijah will come to take him down." 37 Then Jesus gave a loud cry and breathed his last. 38 And the curtain of the temple was torn in two, from top to bottom. 39 Now when the centurion, who stood facing him, saw that in this way he breathed his last, he said, "Truly this man was God's Son!"

40 There were also women looking on from a distance; among them were Mary Magdalene, and Mary the mother of James the younger and of Joses, and Salome. 41 These used to follow him and provided for him when he was in Galilee; and there were many other women who had come up with him to Jerusalem.

"Dear Lord, baby Jesus." That is how fictional NASCAR driver Ricky Bobby in the movie *Talladega Nights* addresses God as he says grace over a meal of "Dominos, KFC and the always delicious Taco Bell."[8] As Ricky goes on and on about baby Jesus, his wife interrupts to remind him that Jesus wasn't just a baby. He did grow up. Ricky responds that he likes the Christmas Jesus best and he is the one saying grace. When it is her turn to pray, she can pray to teenaged Jesus or bearded Jesus or whatever other Jesus she wants. Ricky's best friend chimes in that he likes to think of Jesus as showing up at a party in a tuxedo t-shirt indicating he wants to be formal, but he also likes to have fun. One of Ricky's sons says that he likes to think of Jesus as a ninja fighting off samurai warriors. Things are getting

---

[8] "Will Ferrell is ricky bobby saying grace in Talladega Nights," https://www.youtube.com/watch?v=8HfwnpGDFD8

out of hand, so Ricky Bobby returns to his prayer, "Dear 8 pound, 6 ounce newborn infant Jesus ..."

Now, that might seem like an odd way to begin a sermon on Good Friday. After all, Good Friday is not a day for jokes and jest. It is a solemn affair. It is time to contemplate the death of our Lord on the cross. And yet, I think Ricky Bobby's prayer raises important questions for us, questions that can only be answered on a day such as today.

For unlike the Gospels according to Matthew and Luke, the Gospel of Mark does not trot out the baby book with photos of the infant or the toddler Jesus. No shepherds or stars or magi in Mark. Instead, Mark opens with: "This is the beginning of the gospel of Jesus Christ, the Son of God."[9] Yes, from the very beginning we know who Jesus is. He is the Son of God. This is a royal title. In Mark's day it would have been applied to the Roman emperor, not a Jewish peasant. It carries weight and authority. Yes, from the beginning we know who Jesus is.

However, as we read through this Gospel we notice the title is surprisingly absent. In fact, since that first verse the only ones to use the title "Son of God" are unclean spirits and demons! When they do, Jesus sternly orders them to be quiet.[10] This silencing of the unclean spirits and the lack of use of "Son of God" by the disciples or anyone else has even led some scholars to suggest that Jesus intentionally seeks to hide his true identity. He is the Messiah, but that must remain a secret until the appropriate time.

Well, my friends the time has come. The entire Gospel of Mark has led to this day, to this moment. Darkness covered the land from noon until 3 PM, recalling the moments when God first spoke a creative word. Jesus cries out, "My God, my God, why have you forsaken me?" The bystanders think he is calling for Elijah and try to give him some sour wine in hopes he can hang on long enough for them to see a miracle. Yes, the climax for the story, the moment of Jesus' death on the cross, the moment of our redemption is upon

---

[9] Mark 1:1
[10] Mark 3:11-12

us. Surely someone will speak and finally reveal that this is God's Son.

It should be the disciples, right? They have followed Jesus for three years. They watched Jesus heal and perform miracles. They listened to him teach. Peter, James, and John even saw him transfigured in glory. Surely they will raise their voice. This is God's Son.

But they are silent. In fact they are not even mentioned in these verses. They are completely absent. Those who had pledged to follow Jesus to the end have all fled. Are they risk adverse, overcome by fear, or worried about their own self-preservation? Perhaps all of the above. However, in the moment of crisis, the moment of decision, the moment of Jesus' coronation as king, the disciples are not there.

In her wonderful, and yet painful, book *Everything Happens for a Reason and Other Lies I've Loved*, Duke Divinity School Professor Kate Bowler shares the story of the day she was diagnosed with stage IV colon cancer. The nurse calls her with the test results and says she needs to come to the hospital right away. She calls her husband, then her parents and then she calls her sisters who dutifully sit when asked as she tells them the news. Then she writes:

> My next call finds my friend Katherine in the bleachers of a Vanderbilt football game, and she will immediately get into the car, a state away, screaming into the windshield. When I wake up from surgery she will be there, and my foggy brain will not recall that I never asked her to come. She knew I needed her. She will sleep in the hospital chair beside me, pretending it is comfortable, and using her no-nonsense voice with the nurse who won't bring me ice chips.[11]

Yes, there are moments when we just need someone there who knows who we really are and can speak for us when we do not have the words ourselves.

---

[11] Kate Bowler, *Everything Happens for a Reason and Other Lies I've Loved*, 10.

But in this critical moment, the disciples are not there. In fact, the disciples' collective absence helps to focus the passion story. In the opening episode of chapter 15, a large crowd cries for Pilate to crucify Jesus. The narrative then narrows as despite the soldiers' torture, one remains to help: a passerby named Simon compelled to carry the cross. Finally, on the cross, two insurgents hang beside him and the crowd offers nothing but mockery. The women stand at a distance. The disciples are absent. Jesus' own cry expresses his abandonment. The voice that called him "beloved" at his baptism now appears silent. [12] For us and for our salvation, God came into the world as Jesus Christ. And thus we find that only Jesus himself can truly be "there" on the cross.

However, as Jesus breathes his last, God speaks once more. God speaks not in words heard from the heavens, but with an act in the temple. At the moment of Jesus' death, the curtain in the temple is *schizo*, torn in two. Mark used the word *schizo* before to describe the heavens being torn apart at Jesus' baptism as God comes down.[13] Now Jesus' death complete, no longer hidden behind the shroud, God speaks most clearly as God acts on our behalf. God tears open the barrier between the holy and the mundane. God seeks to meet us face to face. Yes, God is there.

Will someone finally notice? Seeing how Jesus takes his last breath we hear the words for which we have longed, "Surely this man was God's Son." But they are found on the lips of a centurion. He represents the power structure that has dealt with the threat Jesus posed. He is a member of the enemy. Uttered as a representative of that power, the centurion's words might declare a final victory over an insurgent who threatened the peace. Professor Sharyn Dowd suggests, "On the level of the story it is a sarcastic comment on the lips of a jaded professional executioner who has just watched one more Jewish peasant die calling on his God."[14] The centurion's voice is a final blasphemy. He dismisses the one who died so quickly as "God's Son" when everyone knew the only son of God was the

[12] Mark 1:11
[13] Mark 1:10
[14] Sharyn Dowd, *Reading Mark: A Literary and Theological Commentary on the Second Gospel*, 162.

Emperor in Rome. But unbeknownst to the centurion, his confession is ironically true.

My friends, no one who was "there" truly comprehended the significance of the moment. The disciples are absent. The bystanders misunderstand. Even as God breaks through with the silent tearing of the cloth in the temple, a centurion dismisses one more Son of God who has been handled with ease. Perhaps we can begin to understand why Ricky Bobby likes the Christmas baby Jesus better. That's a feel good story. This is just painful.

We do not understand how this one on the cross can be the Son of God. How this one can be the Jesus who saves us? How this one can be the Lord of heaven and earth to whom we pray? We do not have answers on a day like today. As retired United Methodist Bishop Will Willimon puts it:

> Today is a day for simply sitting here and beholding our salvation on the cross. We are to adore, to behold, to gaze upon God's victory, experiencing it rather than understanding it. ...
>
> We wanted him to do something good for us, something great, and he just hangs there, impotent, mocked by the world, naked, exposed, now crying out in agony to the God who was supposed to save, saving by not saving, delivering by not delivering, embracing through forsaking, coming close by being so very different, true power in complete weakness.[15]

My friends, there is no nice and neat ending to a sermon on Good Friday. There is no quick quip to counter the world's desire for baby Jesus and distain for the crucified Christ. The Son of God crucified, dead, and buried. Our sin put him there. His love kept him there.

---

[15] Will Willimon, *Thank God it's Friday: Encountering the Seven Last Words from the Cross*, 47.

And so we wait. There is nothing more that we can do for we cannot save ourselves.

But as those who have known from the beginning that this story is "the Gospel, the good news, of Jesus Christ, the Son of God," we wait with hope.

He Must be Raised from the Dead
John 20:1-10

Easter Sunday

¹ Early on the first day of the week, while it was still dark, Mary Magdalene came to the tomb and saw that the stone had been removed from the tomb. ² So she ran and went to Simon Peter and the other disciple, the one whom Jesus loved, and said to them, "They have taken the Lord out of the tomb, and we do not know where they have laid him." ³ Then Peter and the other disciple set out and went toward the tomb. ⁴ The two were running together, but the other disciple outran Peter and reached the tomb first. ⁵ He bent down to look in and saw the linen wrappings lying there, but he did not go in. ⁶ Then Simon Peter came, following him, and went into the tomb. He saw the linen wrappings lying there, ⁷ and the cloth that had been on Jesus' head, not lying with the linen wrappings but rolled up in a place by itself. ⁸ Then the other disciple, who reached the tomb first, also went in, and he saw and believed; ⁹ for as yet they did not understand the scripture, that he must rise from the dead. ¹⁰ Then the disciples returned to their homes.

It was dark. Not yet even the first glimmer of a sunrise peeking over the hills that morning. A woman, by herself, stumbling over rocks due to the darkness and to her tears. She enters a garden, a graveyard actually. She apparently knows the way to the place where she is going because she does not turn aside. The darkness still barely holding the dawn away, she stops at an unmarked tomb, looks up, and to her horror, she sees the stone has been removed. Turning around she starts to run. She doesn't bother to look in the tomb or to ask anyone what has happened. She simply runs back down the path and into the city to find two others - Simon Peter and the other disciple. Upon finding them she announces, "They have taken the Lord out of the tomb and we do not know where they have laid him!"

According to John, that is the scene in the garden on the first Easter morning. Mary arrives at the tomb while it is still dark and discovers that the stone had been removed. Running to Simon Peter and the other disciple, she speaks the first words of that Easter morning. The words she speaks are not words of faith, words of joy, or words of celebration. No, Mary runs to the disciples and says, "They have taken the Lord out of the tomb and we do not know where they have laid him!" Those are words of terror; words of grief; words of despair; and even words of accusation. Someone has moved the body of Jesus. Someone has stolen the body of Jesus. Someone has robbed this grave. That is the first word we hear on Easter morning according to John.

For the Easter story does not begin with Jesus walking out of the tomb. None of the gospels tell the story in that way. No matter how early the first visitors get to the tomb on the first day of the week – in this case, even before the sunrise - no one gets to see the resurrection. No matter how early they arrive, all they see is an empty tomb, a stone rolled away. So, the questions remain: Where is the body and who has taken it?

Simon Peter and the other disciple, moved by Mary's words, run to the tomb to see for themselves. According to John, Peter had been with Jesus from the beginning, ever since his brother Andrew brought him to Jesus declaring, "We have found the Messiah!" Peter had been with Jesus through it all, often standing out of the crowd, but in the end, he denied his Lord three times. That was the last time Peter was mentioned in this story until now.

The other was unnamed, only known as "the disciple Jesus loved." This disciple first appears later in the gospel, reclining next to Jesus at the Last Supper. He then follows Jesus with Peter to the high priest's house after Jesus' arrest, and is later found standing with Mary, Jesus' mother, at the foot of the cross. It is these two who hear Mary Magdalene's announcement, so they set out running for the tomb to see and investigate for themselves.

Well, the other disciple arrives first; apparently, he ran a bit quicker than Peter. The initial evidence had not changed. The stone was still rolled away and the doorway was still empty. He bent down to look in and saw the linen wrappings lying there – the ones used to wrap a body for burial - but no body. He waited for Peter to arrive before going in to investigate further.

Peter didn't stop. He just went right into the tomb. He too saw the linen wrappings but noticed that the cloth used to wrap the head was not lying with the rest. It was rolled up and placed alone by itself. If someone had simply robbed this grave why would they have bothered to unwrap the body? And then why roll up the cloth for the head by itself. It all seemed careful, intentional, and particular.

By now the other disciple had followed Peter into the tomb, looked around and "believed." It does not say what exactly he believed, but it appears that he believed Mary's testimony that the body was gone. *"For as yet they did not understand the scripture, that he must rise from the dead."* So, they went home. The empty tomb does not inspire belief for the disciples in John's gospel. The empty tomb only serves to heighten grief and tears. They have taken the body of our Lord and we do not know where they have laid him.

Now, if you are familiar with this story, you probably know that it does not end right there. Mary remains at the tomb weeping. She first sees two angels in white before encountering the risen Jesus when he calls her by name. But I stopped our scripture reading for this morning with Peter and the other disciple returning home, not yet understanding that Jesus must rise from the dead. It might seem like an odd place to stop. This is Easter Sunday after all! But I wonder if you and I as 21st century American Christians find ourselves in this story right there. Not with a face to face encounter with the risen Lord, but with questions and wonderings about resurrection.

For we live in a time and a culture that seeks to understand the world through observation; through what we can see, discover, create, investigate, and know. That is why magazines publish stories about the historical Jesus at this time of year. I recently read in *National Geographic* a quite interesting article by a reporter who went to Palestine and Jerusalem to discover "The Real Jesus" by investigating archeological digs and discoveries.[16] Actor Hugh Bonneville, of Downton Abby fame, has a documentary on public

---

[16] Kristen Romey, "The Search for the Real Jesus," *National Geographic*, December 2017, p 30-69.

television right now called *Jesus: Countdown to Calvary* in which he, as one reviewer puts it:

> Does not examine the merits or failings of Christianity. He does not get into question of faith or supernatural belief or the divinity of Jesus. Instead, he and the documentary's makers ... look at the historical, economic and sociological factors that contributed to making Jerusalem a powder keg in the days before Jesus' crucifixion.[17]

Yes, perhaps it has always been the case but our first inclination in the modern world is to seek to understand. We are right there with Peter and the other disciple who went back to their homes, *"For as yet they did not understand the scripture, that he must rise from the dead."*

My friends, let me give you permission to pause this morning ... because resurrection is not primarily about understanding. It really happened, Christ has been raised. No doubt about it. But as Professor Richard Lischer writes:

> If the resurrection were meant to be a historically verifiable occurrence, God wouldn't have performed it in the dark without eyewitnesses. "Were you there when God raised him from the tomb?" the [old] spiritual asks. No, in fact, we were not. No one was. "Resurrection" was an event transacted between God the Father and God the Son by the power of God the Holy Spirit. ... We don't know if it was a typically warm Palestinian morning or unseasonably cool. We don't know if the earth shuddered when he arose or if it was ... still. We don't know what he looked like when he was no longer dead, whether he burst the tomb in glory or came out like Lazarus, slowly

---

[17] "From 'Downton' to Jerusalem: Hugh Bonneville searches for Jesus in new documentary," https://www.usatoday.com/story/life/people/2018/03/16/downton-jerusalem-actor-hugh-bonneville-searches-jesus/432935002/

unwrapping his shroud and squinting with wonder against the dawn.[18]

No one is there for the moment of resurrection. Just like Mary, just like Peter and the other disciple, all we today have is an empty tomb and a missing body.

So, I want to suggest to you this morning, almost 2000 years later, that as long as we spend our time looking for Jesus in the tomb, we will not find him. He is not there!

For there is no doubt that the Christian faith is the story of death and resurrection, but the one in the grave is not Christ – it is you and me. In our scripture text, Peter and the other disciple are the only ones inside the tomb and they do not understand. Despite our best efforts to understand the resurrection and even more our attempts to save ourselves with our minds and our knowledge, we continue to find ourselves mired in the grave. If all we had was our ability to understand, we would be lost for sure. But the good news of the gospel is, as Pastor Nadia Bolz-Weber wrote, "The Christian faith is about how God continues to reach into the graves we dig for ourselves and pull us out, giving us new life, in ways both dramatic and small."[19]

My friends, that is why Christ **_must_** be raised from the dead, because those who need to be raised today are you and me.

Yes, we keep digging graves and Christ keeps pulling us out. My friends, in what graves are you at work this morning? Where do you see no hope?

---

[18] Richard Lischer, "We Have Seen the Lord (John 20:1-18)," https://www.christiancentury.org/article/2012-01/we-have-seen-lord
[19] Nadia Bolz-Weber, *Pastrix,* xviii

Is it in a class at school that makes no sense?

Is it your marriage that seems to be drifting apart?

Is it your teenager who refuses to listen?

Is it your job that seems to be going nowhere?

Is it an illness that occupies your every waking thought?

Is it a loved one whose mind is slipping away?

Is it the aging of your own body?

Is it a culture of violence and death?

Is it a world that seems to be spinning out of control?

Yes, my friends, what graves are you in this morning?

The good news of the gospel is that Christ is risen! He goes before us to meet us in the garden, in a room behind locked doors, in our homes, or anywhere else we might be in this world. Yes, no matter how many graves we keep digging, Christ keeps coming to meet us by pulling us out.

This is good news! This is the best news you have ever heard! As we return to our homes this day, believe the good news of the gospel. There is not just a missing body and an empty tomb. No, Christ is risen! He is risen indeed!

Part 2

I AM: Jesus in His Own Words

I AM the Bread of Life
John 6:35-51

35 Jesus said to them, "I am the bread of life. Whoever comes to me will never be hungry, and whoever believes in me will never be thirsty. 36 But I said to you that you have seen me and yet do not believe. 37 Everything that the Father gives me will come to me, and anyone who comes to me I will never drive away; 38 for I have come down from heaven, not to do my own will, but the will of him who sent me. 39 And this is the will of him who sent me, that I should lose nothing of all that he has given me, but raise it up on the last day. 40 This is indeed the will of my Father, that all who see the Son and believe in him may have eternal life; and I will raise them up on the last day."

41 Then the Jews began to complain about him because he said, "I am the bread that came down from heaven." 42 They were saying, "Is not this Jesus, the son of Joseph, whose father and mother we know? How can he now say, 'I have come down from heaven'?" 43 Jesus answered them, "Do not complain among yourselves. 44 No one can come to me unless drawn by the Father who sent me; and I will raise that person up on the last day. 45 It is written in the prophets, 'And they shall all be taught by God.' Everyone who has heard and learned from the Father comes to me. 46 Not that anyone has seen the Father except the one who is from God; he has seen the Father. 47 Very truly, I tell you, whoever believes has eternal life. 48 I am the bread of life. 49 Your ancestors ate the manna in the wilderness, and they died. 50 This is the bread that comes down from heaven, so that one may eat of it and not die. 51 I am the living bread that came down from heaven. Whoever eats of this bread will live forever; and the bread that I will give for the life of the world is my flesh."

Jesus Christ is my Lord and Savior. That is the fundamental confession of faith, right? Jesus is Lord and Savior. Jesus is Lord - the sovereign, the ruler of our lives. Jesus is Savior — he saves us from our sins and restores us to right relationship with God and one another. Yes, Jesus Christ is my Lord and Savior.

From the beginning the church has used that language to talk about who Jesus is. The apostle Paul calls Jesus "Lord" more than 225 times in his letters. He even writes that no one can say, "Jesus is

Lord" except by the power of the Holy Spirit.[20]   Yes, from the earliest days of scripture, the church has called Jesus "Lord."

So, it may be surprising that Jesus rarely uses that term to refer to himself. He uses it occasionally. Remember just a few weeks ago Jesus sends two disciples to get a donkey from Bethany and tells them that if anyone asks what they are doing they should reply, "The Lord needs it." There are a few other examples, but they are rare. The Gospel writers report that other people call Jesus "Lord," but Jesus does not describe himself in a sovereign, ruler of this world, kind of way.

So, then what about "Savior?" This title is even less likely – only 40 times in the entire Old and New Testaments. It is used only four times in the gospels. The first in the song Mary sings when she visits her cousin Elizabeth during their pregnancies and the second by Zechariah after the birth of his son John.[21]   Then on the night of Jesus' birth, angels announce to the shepherds that "unto you is born in the city of David a Savior, who is the Messiah, the Lord." [22] We get a two for one in that verse. A final reference to Savior is made by the women of Samaria after meeting Jesus in John 4, saying "we know that truly this is the Savior of the world."[23]

Those are the only four occurrences in the gospels. So we do not find the title "Savior" on the lips of Jesus either. Despite the fact that his name literally means "he saves," Jesus never claims that he is the Savior from sins or alienation, or the restorer of relationships or anything else. Other people say Jesus is the Savior, but he does not say it about himself.

All this reminds me of a pivotal text in the Gospel according to Mark, when Jesus asks his disciples "Who do the people say that I am?"[24] They respond that some believe he is John the Baptist or Elijah or one of the prophets. Jesus continues, pressing them directly

---

[20] 1 Corinthians 12:3
[21] Luke 1:47 and 69
[22] Luke 2:11
[23] John 4:42
[24] Mark 8:27-30

with the question, "But who do you say that I am?" It is still the question that all disciples of Jesus, that you and I, must answer.

This morning we are beginning a series of sermons from the Gospel of John which seeks to answer that question by first turning it around. Before we can truly declare who *we* say Jesus is, we need to hear *Jesus* tell us *in his own words* who he is. And if Jesus does not use Lord or Savior to describe himself, what does he say?

Well, in the Gospel of John, seven times, we find Jesus say, "I am ..." It is language reminiscent of God's name given to Moses, YHWH: "I am who I am." Yes, in these texts we find a glimpse of who Jesus really is *in his own words*. And what does he say?

"I am the bread of life;"

"I am the light of the world;"

"I am the gate;"

"I am the good shepherd;"

"I am the resurrection and the life;"

"I am the way, the truth, and the life;"

"I am the vine."

Each week between now and the end of May we are going to explore one of these "I am" statements of Jesus. For as New Testament Scholar NT Wright has written,

> What matters is not just what Jesus can do for you; what matters is who Jesus *is*. Only if you're prepared to be confronted by that in a new way can you begin to understand what he can really do for you, what he really wants to do for you.[25]

---

[25] NT Wright, *John for Everyone, Part 1*, 79.

So, in this season of Easter, this season of resurrection and new life, I invite us to see and encounter Jesus in a new way, in a way that perhaps confronts our established and familiar pictures of him. Yes, he is our Lord and Savior, absolutely. We are not going to lose that! But, what might we discover if we seek to hear Jesus in his own words?

We begin with the first saying, "I am the bread of life." Around the first of the year there was a frequent television commercial for Weight Watchers with Oprah Winfrey in which she practically shouts, "I love bread!" That strikes us as odd for a Weight Watchers commercial because it has been ingrained into our minds that bread and carbs lead to weight gain, not weight loss. We should be eating less bread, not more, right?

Do you realize what a luxury it is to think like that? For the majority of human history, and still for the majority of the world today, the challenge has always been too little bread, not too much. Finding enough bread to survive was a daily struggle. In first century Palestine when Jesus said, "I am the bread of life," the average person would either grow grain on their own or personally know the farmer who did. That farmer worked his or her land, cared for the soil, planted the seeds, watched the sprouts grow, tended the crops and removed the weeds, harvested the grain, and ground it themselves or personally took it to someone who did. Once one had flour, making bread required time and effort – measuring out ingredients, mixing, kneading, and baking.

Now I know there are some wonderful bread makers in this church, but I would guess that today most of us buy our bread at the grocery store. At any store in town, there is an entire aisle devoted just to bread. I walk down the aisle and pick out the loaf I want (checking to be sure it is not blue). I go home, untwist the twist-tie, pull out a slice, and make a sandwich – all without any thought or connection to how this slice of bread ended up sitting on a plate in my kitchen.

When Jesus says, "I am the bread of life," he offers us another lens through which to consider the bread we eat. Jesus is not talking about what we eat just to stay alive; what it takes to get enough energy to last until tomorrow. That kind of food was available to the people of Israel as manna in the wilderness. It temporarily satisfied their physical hunger but they had to gather more every day. That is the bread available to us in the grocery store. It is just temporary.

There is nothing temporary about Jesus as the bread of life. Jesus is inaugurating a new Exodus, a new people of God. As Duke Divinity School theologian Norman Wirzba writes, "The bread that Jesus is ... is food for the *healing, transformation,* and *fulfillment* of life, rather than its mere continuation."[26] Usually when we eat food, if we think about it at all, we think of the food being absorbed into our bodies so that the food becomes a part of us. Jesus is talking about receiving the bread of life, receiving Jesus himself, in such a way that the bread *transforms* us. Eating the bread of life is not the destruction and absorption of Christ, but the entrance of Christ's life into our own. As we eat the bread of life, our life begins to participate in His and we find ourselves changed.

So for Jesus to say that he is the bread of life is not just to say that he is our nourishment or even that he provides what we need just for this day. No, "I am the bread of life" means that Jesus is the one at work transforming lives and the world through his presence. To eat the bread of life is to be invited into eternal life. Again NT Wright says,

> It is another way of saying what the [first chapter of John] said: Jesus is the Word, the one who comes from the Father into the world to accomplish his purpose. And in this case the particular emphasis is on nourishment. Until they recognize who Jesus really is, they may be fed with bread and fish, but there is a deep hunger inside them which will never be satisfied. [Sir, give us this bread always] can be used to this day, as it stands, as the prayer that we all need to pray if our deepest needs are to be met. ... The entire story John is telling is designed to end with Jesus pioneering the way into [a] newly embodied life, and the promise of the present

---

[26] Norman Wirzba, *Food and Faith: A Theology of Eating*, 155.

chapter is that this life will be shared by all who taste the living bread.[27]

So, my friends, as we end today we come back to the question we will ask throughout this series: Who do you say Jesus is? For more than merely a Lord, more than merely a Savior – Jesus is the bread of life, the pioneer of a new life in which our deepest hungers might be filled. Do you believe this?

---

[27] Wright, 81.

I AM the Light of the World
John 9:1-12

[1] As he walked along, he saw a man blind from birth. [2] His disciples asked him, "Rabbi, who sinned, this man or his parents, that he was born blind?" [3] Jesus answered, "Neither this man nor his parents sinned; he was born blind so that God's works might be revealed in him. [4] We must work the works of him who sent me while it is day; night is coming when no one can work. [5] As long as I am in the world, I am the light of the world." [6] When he had said this, he spat on the ground and made mud with the saliva and spread the mud on the man's eyes, [7] saying to him, "Go, wash in the pool of Siloam" (which means Sent). Then he went and washed and came back able to see. [8] The neighbors and those who had seen him before as a beggar began to ask, "Is this not the man who used to sit and beg?" [9] Some were saying, "It is he." Others were saying, "No, but it is someone like him." He kept saying, "I am the man." [10] But they kept asking him, "Then how were your eyes opened?" [11] He answered, "The man called Jesus made mud, spread it on my eyes, and said to me, 'Go to Siloam and wash.' Then I went and washed and received my sight." [12] They said to him, "Where is he?" He said, "I do not know."

Do you remember how the entire story of scripture begins? All the way back in the book of Genesis? Yes, in the beginning when God began to create the heavens and the earth, the earth was a formless void and darkness covered the face of the deep while the Spirit of God swept over the waters. Then God said, "Let there be light!" and there was light.[28]

Now, I certainly was not there when all this creating and calling happened, but in my mind's eye I suspect that this light God called into being was not just the flare of a match. Not just a spark. Not just a candle flicker in the wind. No, this was LIGHT! Overwhelming, awe-inspiring, blind your eyes, take your breath away LIGHT!

In the Gospel of John, as he recounts Jesus' life and ministry, John loves to employ the metaphor of light and its contrast with darkness.

---

[28] Genesis 1:1-5

Perhaps you remember from the opening chapter of the Gospel of John:

> In the beginning was the Word, and the Word was with God, and the Word was God. All things came into being through him, and without him not one thing came into being. What has come into being in him was life and the life was the light of all people. And the light shines in the darkness and the darkness does not overcome it.[29]

Perhaps because it is when I read that text every year, but I imagine a Christmas Eve candlelight service when I hear these opening verses of the Gospel of John. Can you picture that in your mind? The lights are dim, the Advent wreath flickers with five solitary candles. The light seems to push back the darkness ever so slightly. But the darkness threatens. Then the light begins to be shared. From one person to another, one pew after another, slowly the light spreads, the darkness retreats into the corners of the room, and it is replaced by a soft glow. It is nice and warm and comforting.

But what if John intends for us to think not of the nice and sweet candlelight of Christmas Eve, but instead of God calling forth light at the beginning of creation? In the beginning there was LIGHT! It was dramatic and powerful. It threw back the chaos; it banished the darkness; it shattered the deep. Suddenly, life is possible. What if that is what John has in mind? What has come into being was life and the life was the light of all people! Not just a flicker, not just a candle in the wind, but the light, the transformation, new creation of all people! The darkness is not just held at bay; it is defeated and banished for the light has come.

Yes, I wonder if that is what John had in mind. And if so, it changes how I hear our text for today as well. For this is not just a simple healing story. This is a revelation story – a glimpse into the creative power of God to make all things new. For this darkness

---

[29] John 1:1-5

transforming, status quo upsetting, light of the world has come and it has a name – Jesus.

Jesus is walking along and encounters a man who has been blind from birth. The disciples are interested in the cause and effect. Blindness must be the result of sin, right? So who sinned, him or his parents?

But Jesus is not interested in that question and we should not let it sidetrack us this morning either. As biblical scholar Lamar Williamson writes,

> Jesus … changes the man's blindness from a result to a possibility – an occasion for the revelation of God's glorious work. Neither Jesus nor the evangelist is interested in speculations about where sin and darkness come from. The world is blind and God's work is to heal it.[30]

Yes, as Jesus tells the first disciples, "We must work the works of him who sent me while it is day … as long as I am in the world, "I am the light of the world."

Jesus first made that claim, that he is the light of the world, back in chapter 8. But there it almost comes just in passing related to a festival with an emphasis on lights. But here, what it means to be the light of the world is enacted as a revelation, as a new creation.

Once again with echoes of the first chapters of Genesis, we find Jesus at work in the mud, crafting something new. In Genesis God created Adam, a creature of earth, and breathed life into him. Here, Jesus is creating something new – sight through new eyes we might say - by spitting into the mud, making a paste, and putting it on the man's eyes. He tells him to go and wash in the pool with the name "Sent." The man does and once again, from the water emerges a new creation. For "the man went and washed and came back able to see."

---

[30] Lamar Williamson, *Preaching the Gospel of John*, 110.

Yes, this darkness transforming, status quo upsetting, light of the world enables the blind to see. And those who now see are not just those who have lost their sight through some act of the will or some accident. No, those who have never seen before get new eyes. The light brings a new creation enacted and envisioned by Jesus himself.

However, not everyone finds this new creation easy to understand or welcome. Most of the verses we read today and the vast majority of the rest of the chapter are the man's friends and then the Pharisees and leaders trying to figure out if the man who now sees is the same man who had been born blind. The man repeatedly echoes the words of Jesus, declaring, "I am." And yet, they still do not believe. They find every excuse possible not to believe – from the fact that the healing happened on the Sabbath to their belief that not since creation itself has someone born blind been healed. They refuse to see what the light of the world reveals to them. Despite the darkness transforming, status quo upsetting, light of the world new creation, people continue to love darkness.

And the darkness does not go down without a fight. In John's Gospel, Jesus is moving quickly to Jerusalem and the cross that awaits. Jesus says, "I am the light of the world." Jesus is the light that not just flickers, but transforms, that creates, and banishes the darkness. The darkness will threaten once again, but even on the cross the light still shines.

We had an experience like that here at Reid Memorial just over a year ago. At our Maundy Thursday service we used 120 small tea lights on a little table with a glass cover. We placed the lights on the table to create a marvelous cross. The tea lights were supposed to burn for four hours, much longer than we needed, so I decided that we would light all of the candles just before the service began. They would burn throughout the service and then at the conclusion, as everyone departed in silence, each person would come forward and extinguish a single candle.

It was a stunning display and visual image as the service progressed. The lit candles reflected off the glass, doubling the effect of the cross. However, as we reached communion, the candles having burned for about 45 minutes at this point, something happened. Either the Holy Spirit or the air conditioning – I can't say for sure which one – kicked on. And the moving air caused those tea lights to flare up. Especially in the middle of the cross where there was a concentration of heat and built up wax, the candles began to overflow, joining their flames together. Suddenly we had a fire. It wasn't what I'd call a blaze, but it was on the way. Faithful elders on the worship committee stepped forward and with small snuffers attempted to extinguish the growing flames. It appeared to be a losing battle as the heat grew hotter as the flames flickered higher.

Suddenly the glass table top cracked with a loud crash. I was in the midst of the Great Prayer of Thanksgiving and the shattered glass startled me, but I just kept praying. With perseverance and a little grace, the flames gradually were brought under control.

I share that story with you not because I intend to ever create such a cross out of tea lights again. No, we learned our lesson on that one. I share it with you because in an unexpected and yet powerful way it reminds us of the light that even the darkness of the cross cannot contain. For the darkness transforming, status quo upsetting, uncontrollable light of the world has come. And this light has a name – Jesus. In the healing of a man born blind he reveals that the same light and power that burst into the world on the very first day can touch even you and me.

My friends can you see him? Who do you say that Jesus is? Can you claim that he is the light of the world? Not just a spark or a candle in the wind, but the power and presence of a new creation that might heal even our blindness? Do you believe this?

I AM the Gate and the Good Shepherd
John 10:7-18

7 So again Jesus said to them, "Very truly, I tell you, I am the gate for the sheep. 8 All who came before me are thieves and bandits; but the sheep did not listen to them. 9 I am the gate. Whoever enters by me will be saved, and will come in and go out and find pasture. 10 The thief comes only to steal and kill and destroy. I came that they may have life, and have it abundantly.

11 "I am the good shepherd. The good shepherd lays down his life for the sheep. 12 The hired hand, who is not the shepherd and does not own the sheep, sees the wolf coming and leaves the sheep and runs away—and the wolf snatches them and scatters them. 13 The hired hand runs away because a hired hand does not care for the sheep. 14 I am the good shepherd. I know my own and my own know me, 15 just as the Father knows me and I know the Father. And I lay down my life for the sheep. 16 I have other sheep that do not belong to this fold. I must bring them also, and they will listen to my voice. So there will be one flock, one shepherd. 17 For this reason the Father loves me, because I lay down my life in order to take it up again. 18 No one takes it from me, but I lay it down of my own accord. I have power to lay it down, and I have power to take it up again. I have received this command from my Father."

There was once a pastor taking a group of parishioners on a tour of the Holy Land. As often happens on such trips, the pastor attempted to make connections between the scriptures and actual places they would see and people the group might encounter.

On this particular day, as the bus departed the hotel, the pastor read the parable of the good shepherd and explained to them that as they continued their tour, they would see shepherds on the hillsides just as in Jesus' day.

He wanted to impress the group, so he told them what every good pastor tells his people about shepherds. He described how, in the Holy Land, shepherds always lead their sheep, always walking in front to face dangers, always protecting the sheep by going ahead of them.

He barely got the last word out when, sure enough, the bus rounded a corner and they saw a man and his sheep on the hillside.

There was only one problem: the man wasn't leading the sheep as the good pastor had said. No, he was behind the sheep and seemed to be chasing them. The pastor's face turned a bright red.

Flabbergasted, he made the bus stop. He jumped out and ran over to the field and said, "I always thought shepherds in this region led their sheep — out in front. And I told my people that a good shepherd never chases his sheep."

The man chasing the sheep stopped and replied, "That's absolutely true ... you're absolutely right ... but I'm not a shepherd, I'm the butcher!"

Yes, my friends, it is important to be able to recognize the good shepherd because there are multiple other options out there.

I believe that our scripture today is about Jesus and leadership and the kind of leader who can take the sheep to a life that really is life. Think with me just for a minute about leaders and leadership in today's world. There are a variety of models which are held up as examples for leadership. On the one hand there is the corporate CEO who works in an office. Today they either wear a suit or (if they are in the technology industry) jeans, a t-shirt, and a hoodie. Either way, they spend most of their time in meetings, rarely getting their hands dirty or involved in the actual production or operations of the company. They are accountable to shareholders and a corporate board. And how do we know if a particular CEO is an outstanding leader? If the business makes money, of course; especially if it makes more money every quarter than is expected.

There are other models of leadership too. In the political realm we tend to lift up those who are steadfast to the party and its principles. No flip flopping, right? They must not compromise with the other side of the aisle. If their greatest accomplishment is not letting the other side win, they must be a good leader, right?

In the athletic arena, coaches and players are often lifted up as good leaders. What criteria do we use here? Winning games, developing players who win at the current level and the next. Nice guys finish last and don't write best-selling books about leadership.

Now perhaps there are other models for leadership which you appreciate. And I am sure there are those in the corporate, political, and sports worlds which do not fit the description I just provided. However, it does seem true to me that the majority of leaders we tend to celebrate look very little like the shepherd we find in the scriptures.

And that is a problem because "shepherd" is the dominant metaphor used in the both the Old and the New Testaments to talk about the ideal leader. Moses was keeping his father-in-law's sheep when he encountered God on Mt. Sinai. King David, a king after God's own heart, was a shepherd. The psalms are full of references to shepherds, as in Psalm 23 which we read this morning. And perhaps most important for our text today, the prophets critique the kings of Israel for not being good shepherds. For example, in Ezekiel 34 we hear:

> Prophesy against the shepherds of Israel; prophesy and say to them … Ah you shepherds of Israel who have been feeding yourselves! Should not shepherds feed the sheep? … You have not strengthened the weak, you have not healed the sick, you have not bound up the injured, you have not brought back the strayed, you have not sought the lost, but with force and harshness you have ruled them.[31]

Yes, the shepherd is the model for good leadership in scripture, and even more than just any leader, the king should be a good shepherd.

All of this is in the background of our text for today when Jesus declares first that he is the gate and then that he is the good shepherd. Both images are related to the king's task of keeping sheep.

---

[31] Ezekiel 34:2-4

For it was not unusual for shepherds to lead their flocks to a pen or sheep fold for the night. Such places had low walls and a single open entry way. As opposed to having a gate that swings back and forth like we might have in our yards today, the shepherd would often lay across the entryway at night. He was the gate - the one who kept the thieves and wolves out, the one who kept the sheep safely in. When Jesus says, "I am the gate," he declares that he is the means by which the sheep enter the safety of the sheep fold. He is the means by which the sheep exit for the abundant life promised in the pastures.

So, Jesus is already talking about being a shepherd when he says that he is the gate. However, you can almost see people scratching their heads, so Jesus continues, spelling it out for them: "I am the good shepherd." The word we translate as "good" is the Greek word *kalos*. We often tell children they are supposed to be good and by that we mean they are to act appropriately and morally. But *kalos* means more than just something or someone who follows the rules. No, *kalos* is often translated as noble or beautiful or proper or even praise worthy. So, if one is the *kalos* shepherd, then he or she is the role model, the archetype, the one whose picture is in the dictionary beside the word. Yes, this shepherd is something special indeed. This is the shepherd God wanted the kings of Israel to be. This is the shepherd that God said he himself would be because the kings of Israel keep failing so miserably.

The contrast is with the hired hand, the one who watches the sheep for money. When the wolf comes, the hired hand leaves the sheep and runs away. But the good shepherd, the *kalos* shepherd, fights off the wolves with a great show of strength, right? No! The noble shepherd *lays down his life* for the sheep. He is the king who truly cares for the people. To paraphrase the words from Ezekiel, when the wolves come the good shepherd strengthens the weak, heals the sick, binds up the injured, brings back the strayed, and seeks the lost. Yes, this shepherd will unite and care for his sheep by laying down his life for them.

Now, we know this story ends with crucifixion and resurrection; but just imagine hearing that for the first time. The shepherd will lay down his life for the sheep? What good would that do? A dead shepherd is no better than a hired hand that runs off. In either case the sheep are left alone and defenseless.

Is that not exactly where the disciples and the followers of Jesus must have been on the days following Good Friday. Jesus, their good shepherd, who they had followed into the mouth of danger itself, Jerusalem, had laid down his life. But what good was that? They were now without a shepherd, they had scattered in fear, and those that put Jesus to death sought his followers to make sure they did not cause any trouble on their own. It would have been just the same as if they had a hired hand that had fled at the first sight of danger. The outcome was the same. They were scattered, scared, and alone. What sense does it make for a shepherd to lay down his life for the sheep?

It only makes sense if the shepherd who lays down his life, also takes it up again. As Jesus says, "No one takes my life from me, but I lay it down of my own accord. I have power to lay it down, and I have power to take it up again." Jesus is the *kalos* shepherd, the good shepherd not only because he lays down his life for the sheep, but also because he picks his life back up again. He does not leave the sheep without a shepherd, scattered and snatched in fear. The hired hand flees, never to return. The good shepherd lays down his life for the sheep, conquers the enemy of death, and then picks his life back up again to lead the sheep through green pastures and beside still waters.

And that, my friends, brings us back to our essential question: Who do you say that Jesus is? Because Jesus is calling to you and to me. Do you recognize his voice? He is the *kalos* shepherd, the good shepherd who guards us against the threats of night and leads us forth into the pastures of abundant life. When the wolves of life appear, threatening to scatter and snatch us, Jesus lays down his life for us – gives his life so that we might live, knowing that we cannot fight off the wolves on our own. And yet in laying down his life, he does not abandon us, but takes his life up again so that we will always know this good shepherd. Do you believe this?

I AM the Resurrection and the Life
John 11:17-27

17 When Jesus arrived, he found that Lazarus had already been in the tomb four days. 18 Now Bethany was near Jerusalem, some two miles away, 19 and many of the Jews had come to Martha and Mary to console them about their brother. 20 When Martha heard that Jesus was coming, she went and met him, while Mary stayed at home. 21 Martha said to Jesus, "Lord, if you had been here, my brother would not have died. 22 But even now I know that God will give you whatever you ask of him." 23 Jesus said to her, "Your brother will rise again." 24 Martha said to him, "I know that he will rise again in the resurrection on the last day." 25 Jesus said to her, "I am the resurrection and the life. Those who believe in me, even though they die, will live, 26 and everyone who lives and believes in me will never die. Do you believe this?" 27 She said to him, "Yes, Lord, I believe that you are the Messiah, the Son of God, the one coming into the world."

Have you ever found yourself not sure what to say to someone who's loved one has died? It is the same if the person has just been diagnosed with something dreadful, isn't it? After the hug or handshake in the receiving line at the funeral home, or when seeing a friend in the aisle at the grocery store, or arriving with a dish of food, what we do we say?

In that moment of awkwardness or loss, sometimes we fall back on clichés or empty platitudes. Duke Divinity School professor Kate Bowler has heard them all after being diagnosed with stage-4 colon cancer at the age of 35. She writes:

> Most everyone I meet is dying to make me certain. They want me to know, without a doubt, that there is a hidden logic to this seeming chaos. Even when I was still in the hospital, a neighbor came to the door and told my husband that everything happens for a reason.

> "I'd love to hear it," he replied.

> "Pardon?" she said, startled.

"The reason my wife is dying," he said in that sweet and sour way he has, effectively ending the conversation as the neighbor stammered something and handed him a casserole.[32]

In fact, Bowler heard that one so often that it became the name of her recent memoir - a haunting, truthful, painful, and ultimately beautiful book called *Everything Happens for a Reason and Other Lies I've Loved.*

In our text for today I get the sense that Martha has heard about all the reasons and clichés and platitudes that she can stand when Jesus finally shows up. She had sent word in plenty of time, but he comes several days late. That's the biting part of her greeting, right? "Lord, if you had been here, my brother would not have died." No, "thank you for coming." No, "we are doing as well as can be expected." No, "we have plenty of food from the friends who came down from Jerusalem for the funeral." Instead of offering a platitude of her own Martha says, "Lord, if you had been here, my brother would not have died."

Jesus responds, "Your brother will rise again."

Really? That is the best Jesus can do? Martha had heard them all by this point. So, she responds based on what she thinks she heard Jesus say. What she heard was something like: "You will see him again someday." Martha is still convinced that if Jesus had been there, her brother would not have died. So, she says, "Sure, Jesus, all the Pharisees back at the house told me that, I know that he will rise on the last day with everyone else."

Now we should note that belief in a general resurrection at the end of time was a fairly new theological development in first century Palestine. New Testament scholar Alan Culpepper writes,

> The Greeks believed in the immortality of the human soul, that there is something in the human being that is inherently

---

[32] Kate Bowler, *Everything Happens for a Reason and Other Lies I've Loved*, 112-113.

immortal. But the Hebrew belief was that there is nothing inherently immortal in the human soul. Life beyond death depends entirely on God and the power of God. ... So recent was this belief that not all first-century Jews had accepted it. The Pharisees and the Essenes believed in the resurrection of the dead, but the Sadducees did not.[33]

So, Martha is already making a theological move here to say that yes, she would see her brother again - on the last day with the resurrection of everyone.

But that is not what Jesus has in mind. Jesus isn't talking about some day in the future, some moment a long time from now when the kingdom comes, a day to be determined when we'll all fly away. No, Jesus is talking about today, about now, about this place, about this time, about this body lying in a tomb for four days, so dead that it's started to stink. Yes, Jesus is talking about the circumstances of this world, of this life, of your life and mine. "I am the resurrection and the life" he declares and he really means it. Not someday, somewhere else. Today, this day, "I am the resurrection and the life ... Do you believe this?"

And that is the question, isn't it? You might have noticed I have asked you that question at the end of each of the sermons in this series. Do you believe this? Do you believe there is a force at work in the world more powerful than the forces of power, money, race, violence, and death? Do you believe that even the most hopeless circumstances are not without hope? Do you believe that even a body so dead that it stinks can rise? Do you believe that tragedies and losses of the past and the present do not have to dictate the future? Do you believe that there is another way, a way that leads to life? Just as he asked Martha so many years ago, with so much more than clichés and platitudes, Jesus says to you and to me, "I am the resurrection and the life. Not just someday in the future, but today. Do you believe this?"

---

[33] R. Alan Culpepper, *The Gospel and Letters of John*, 185.

My friends, resurrection can never be an empty platitude. For as scholar NT Wright has said, "Resurrection isn't just a doctrine. It isn't just a future fact. It's a *person* and here he is standing in front of Martha, teasing her to make the huge leap of trust and hope."[34]

It is the leap we are all invited to make as we seek to know who Jesus really is. In the face of all of all the clichés and platitudes, Kate Bowler writes of her struggle to see Jesus today:

> I can't reconcile the way that the world is jolted by events that are wonderful and terrible, the gorgeous and the tragic. Except I am beginning to believe that these opposites do not cancel each other out. … Joy persists somehow and I soak it in. The horror of cancer has made everything seem like it is painted in bright colors. I think the same thoughts again and again: Life is beautiful. Life is so hard.[35]

Life is beautiful. Life is so hard. That is what Jesus brings when he shows up and declares "I am the resurrection and the life." He is saying that in him the world is not stuck in the tragedies of the past. In him the future worries and all our grand plans fade away. He stands in the middle, arms stretched wide, crucified and risen, so that in him, in the present moment, we might see the world painted in bright colors. For all we really have, all any of us really have, is today.

Thus, Kate Bowler concludes her book with these words:

> My little plans are crumbs scattered on the ground. This is all I have learned about living here, plodding along and finding God. My well-laid plans are no longer my foundation. I can only hope that my dreams, my actions, my hopes are leaving a trail for [my son] Zach and [my husband] Toban, so, whichever way the path turns, all they will find is Love.
>
> Zach is beside me in our big bed as I write these words, rolling around like a polar bear cub. After we take him out

---

[34] NT Wright, *John for Everyone, Volume 2,* 7.
[35] Bowler, 123.

of his crib in the morning he loves to come "up-up" to our loft bedroom and loll around like only two-year-olds can. It's another beautiful morning, and it's time to yell with the pitch of the coffee grinder and make him French toast. I will die, yes, but not today.[36]

My friends, who do say that Jesus is? He declares in his own words, "I am the resurrection and the life." He is with us, here and now. Whether we speak or whether we are silent, he is our hope and our God so that we might live today. Do you believe this?

---

[36] Ibid, 165-166.

I AM the Way, the Truth, and the Life
John 14:1-7

¹ "Do not let your hearts be troubled. Believe in God, believe also in me. ² In my Father's house there are many dwelling places. If it were not so, would I have told you that I go to prepare a place for you? ³ And if I go and prepare a place for you, I will come again and will take you to myself, so that where I am, there you may be also. ⁴ And you know the way to the place where I am going." ⁵ Thomas said to him, "Lord, we do not know where you are going. How can we know the way?" ⁶ Jesus said to him, "I am the way, and the truth, and the life. No one comes to the Father except through me. ⁷ If you know me, you will know my Father also. From now on you do know him and have seen him."

There was once a great cartoon in *The New Yorker* magazine that depicts a pastor standing at a crossroads where he is clearly struggling with which path to choose. At the intersection is a signpost with two signs. One has an arrow and points to "Heaven." The second sign points down the other road to "Discussion about Heaven." So, Heaven or Discussion about Heaven? It is an anguish-filled choice.

After mentioning this cartoon in one of her books, Pastor Lillian Daniel writes:

> Sometimes I think we in the church stand at the same crossroads, stuck between "Jesus" and "Discussions about Jesus." This is particularly true of thoughtful, intelligent people who are not afraid to ask questions about the Bible and the history and culture of Jesus' day. We are so comfortable that we are better at articulating what we do not believe about Jesus intellectually than saying what we do believe about him personally.

But also stuck are the people who claim to know exactly who Jesus is, and then use that as a test to see if everyone else is saved or unsaved.[37]

It seems to me this is part of the challenge with a text like today's sixth "I AM" statement of Jesus. "I AM the way, and the truth, and the life. No one comes to the Father except through me." We are tempted, just like the disciples were, to try to figure out where Jesus is going; how in the world we are not supposed to be troubled at his departure; and even how many rooms are there really in that mansion in the Father's house.

And all that thinking about someplace else leads us to begin debating who else is going to be there (because we are confident that we will be there, right?). Perhaps you have heard or even participated in these debates before:

> 1. This text is exclusive because Jesus is *the* way, *the* truth, and *the* life. There is no other name, no other way, no other truth that leads to the Father. We have this truth and others don't. It's like one of the golden tickets in *Willy Wonka and the Chocolate Factory*. If you find one you get inside the candy factory. If you don't you are left outside. So you better get a ticket because while God is for us, God is against you and unless you too accept Jesus as your Lord and Savior, become a Christian, and join the church (and even better join *our* church) you are not going to like the end of your story.

> 2. Now that may strike us as 21st century Americans as a bit harsh. After all there are many other religions out there. So, perhaps this text is not exclusive, but pluralistic. Yes, we can add, *"for us Christians"* Jesus is the way, the truth, and the life. After all he was just talking about his disciples here, those who already knew him, not about the whole world. As Christians, *we* know

---

[37] Lillian Daniel, *When "Spiritual But Not Religious" is not Enough: Seeing God in Surprising Places, Even the Church*, 157-158.

the saving work of God in Jesus Christ, but others may find the same thing in other religious figures. No need to judge or be intolerant. We are all really just trying to find our way to God through different paths.

3. Now, that may sound like we have thrown the baby Jesus out with the bathwater in an attempt to not offend anyone. So, still others read this text not as exclusive or pluralistic but as inclusive. Yes, Christianity is the true, unique, and definitive religion but God's grace is also at work outside the Christian circle, often in ways and in people who do not recognize Jesus. One does not really need to know Jesus or call on his name to be saved because like a rising tide that lifts all boats, through Jesus as the way, the truth, and the life everyone has been saved – even if they don't know it yet. [38]

Do you see how these "discussions about Jesus" threaten to pull us in like the sirens beckoning unsuspecting sailors to shipwreck on a rocky coast?

Yes, we are threatened with shipwreck because did you notice that all three of those attempts to understand this text and its relation to non-Christians are not about Jesus at all. All three are about us: what *we* think, what *we* fear, or what *we* hope. Yes, the farther we travel down the "discussions about Jesus" road the farther we get from the question that has guided this entire series: Who do you say that Jesus is?

I think that should be the guiding interpretative question for this text. Who do you say that Jesus is? In his own words Jesus says, "I am the way, the truth, and the life. No one comes to the Father except through me." Throughout this series we have seen that Jesus is not talking about himself in some future way or about how he will be in some other place. No, Jesus is talking about himself here and

---

[38] These three descriptions of the exclusivist, pluralistic, and inclusive positions are roughly based on Shirley Guthrie, *Always Being Reformed: Faith for a Fragmented World*, 63-65.

now, in the present tense, the Word made flesh and living among us. So here and now who do we say that Jesus is? As he reflected on this text, the late theologian Shirley Guthrie of Columbia Theological Seminary answered the question this way:

> Who is the one whom Christians confess to be the way, the truth, and the life? According to the New Testament, he is the expression of God's love not just for Christian believers but for all humanity, the one in whom God was at work to reconcile *the whole world* to himself. He came not to give his followers everything they wanted to be happy, successful, and secure now and forever, but to announce and usher in the worldwide reign of God's justice and compassion for *everyone*. He was the friend not just of law-abiding, God-fearing insiders, but of sinful, unbelieving, or different-believing outsiders. He believed that caring for suffering and needy human beings was more important than conformity to the moral and theological requirements of religious orthodoxy. He came not to condemn, defeat, and lord it over those who rejected him but to give his life for them, to restore to them their own true humanity and to reconcile them to God and their fellow human beings. And God raised *him* from the dead and made *him* to be the crucified and risen Lord over all principalities and authorities everywhere – not just Lord over the church or Lord in the hearts of Christians, but risen Lord who continues his healing, reconciling, liberating, saving work everywhere in the world. Even where he is not yet known, acknowledged and served; even before Christians get there to tell others about him.[39]

My friends, do you begin to see that this text is about the way, the truth, and the life that is not a doctrine or a ticket to heaven but a person? It is not about us. It is about Jesus. Yes, it is about Jesus - a person who meets our deepest hungers, who brings the creative and life transforming power of God into a new creation, who rules this

---

[39] Ibid, 69-70.

new creation as a shepherd, and who brings the new life of resurrection to us – *all of this here and now!*

He is the one we seek, he is the mystery of grace, he is the one who died for us, who rose for us, and who will come again for us. The rest is mere speculation. All we can do is point to Jesus. For only in him is there salvation, for us and our neighbors. Do you believe this?

I AM the True Vine

John 15:1-11

¹ "I am the true vine, and my Father is the vinegrower. ² He removes every branch in me that bears no fruit. Every branch that bears fruit he prunes to make it bear more fruit. ³ You have already been cleansed by the word that I have spoken to you. ⁴ Abide in me as I abide in you. Just as the branch cannot bear fruit by itself unless it abides in the vine, neither can you unless you abide in me. ⁵ I am the vine, you are the branches. Those who abide in me and I in them bear much fruit, because apart from me you can do nothing. ⁶ Whoever does not abide in me is thrown away like a branch and withers; such branches are gathered, thrown into the fire, and burned. ⁷ If you abide in me, and my words abide in you, ask for whatever you wish, and it will be done for you. ⁸ My Father is glorified by this, that you bear much fruit and become my disciples. ⁹ As the Father has loved me, so I have loved you; abide in my love. ¹⁰ If you keep my commandments, you will abide in my love, just as I have kept my Father's commandments and abide in his love. ¹¹ I have said these things to you so that my joy may be in you, and that your joy may be complete.

Today is a day of transition. It is the last day of a sermon series. This is the Sunday of Memorial Day Weekend, so it is the unofficial beginning of summer. Even more it is a weekend for remembering those who have given their lives in the service of their country. So yes, today is an appropriate day for us to do a bit of reflection.

A few years ago, in an email to his congregation, Pastor Scott Black Johnson of Fifth Avenue Presbyterian Church in New York City used the following questions to encourage his congregation to engage in just this kind of moment of reflection about their faith. He wrote:

> Go somewhere quiet -- somewhere you will not be interrupted. Close your eyes. Now, take the pulse of your soul. Ask yourself, "How would I describe the current state of my faith?"

> As you consider the question, try to be specific and candid. Choose the most fitting, most honest adjectives.

- Is my faith growing, or shrinking?
- Is it engaged, or yawning?
- Is it mystical, or highly rational?
- Is it far in the background of my daily life, or a clear lamp on my path?
- Is my faith stuck in a rut, or is it changing?
- Is the way I relate to Christianity, the Bible and the hymns of the church different than it was a year ago? Ten years ago?[40]

My friends, I encourage you to spend some time this weekend or in this week ahead taking the pulse of your soul. How would you describe the current state of your faith? Or to use the language of our scripture text for today – are you bearing fruit?

Because in his final "I AM" statement in the Gospel according to John, Jesus says, "I am the true vine and you are the branches." He then continues with what can sound like a threat: "Abide in me, "bear fruit," or be pruned, wither, be thrown into the fire, and die! Maybe I have watched too many mob movies in my life, but I think if we are not careful, we can hear Jesus' words in this text like a mob boss threatening the disciples into remaining loyal even though Jesus is "going away for a while."

But if we listen carefully, we discover that Jesus does not just say, "Abide in me." Instead he says: "Abide in me *as I abide in you.*" As pastor David Lose has written:

> That changes everything. The other statements about pruning and withering and the rest are not threats of intimidation but rather statements of fact, descriptions of what happens when we do not abide in Jesus, when we are separated from his love and acceptance, when we run or hide or think we can do it on our own or decide to stand

[40] Scott Black Johnson, "Dear Friends in Christ," http://campaign.r20.constantcontact.com/render?m=1103640741121&ca=72b938ce-3bd8-49eb-a493-225a8f4b9b3c

alone or whatever. Branches don't do that well when separated from the vine. At best they, like cut flowers, have a burst of color and bloom but then fade and wither.[41]

So, it is not a threat when Jesus talks about the branches withering and being thrown to the fire. It is an invitation to abide in him as he abides in us. Now, I know that "abide" is not a word that we use all that much anymore. In Greek the word is *meno* which means to stay, last, endure, live with, remain, or dwell. So, to abide in Christ means to live with or dwell with Christ over the long haul. And we recognize that to live with someone not just for a day or two, but to dwell with another is pretty close. You know that the people you dwell with know just about everything there is to know about you. They know what your hair looks like when you first wake up in the morning. They know if you are the one who wakes up without an alarm, with an alarm, with just a couple of snoozes on the alarm, or with more than a couple of snoozes on that alarm. They are the ones who know your favorite foods and those things that you cannot even stand the smell of. They are the ones who know about your pet peeves and the things that really annoy you. The ones you abide with are the ones who know how much money you have in the bank. They know your deepest struggles and your deepest fears. Yes, that is pretty close. And Jesus says, "Abide in me and I in you."

I believe that all of us today in the midst of our American culture are looking for a place to abide; a place to land; a place to rest. We struggle with the daily demands of life, work, and families. We go to bed tired, we wake up tired, and trudge through our days tired. We are searching for that place where we can truly dwell and find the rest that we so desperately need. So often our culture encourages us to find that "rest" in stuff. If you have a bigger TV then you will enjoy the game more on Sunday afternoons. If you have a bigger car then you can rest as you sit in traffic because in your mind you will be cruising the open road. If you have enough money in the bank you can retire early and rest through your 50's and 60's. We are

---

[41] David Lose, "Easter 5B: As I Abide in You," http://www.davidlose.net/2018/04/easter-5-b-as-i-abide-in-you/?utm_source=feedburner&utm_medium=email&utm_campaign=Feed%3A+davidlose%2FIsqE+%28...In+the+Meantime%29

seeking a place to abide, to rest, and our culture says that if we accumulate enough stuff then we will be happy. And yet, somehow no matter how much we stuff we get, we never find the rest it promises.

All this brings us back to Jesus' "I am" statement in this text. "I am the vine and you are the branches." As the vine grows, so do the branches that abide in it. For branches abide in the vine. If we Christians have any hope of "bearing fruit," "keeping commandments," and "glorifying God," then the first step is to take a step back, to stop our busyness, and to abide in Christ, remembering that abiding in Christ does not just mean sitting on a lounge chair with some sweet tea. No abiding in Christ means to go where he goes and to be where he is – meeting deepest hungers, bringing light into darkness, giving his life for the world, and showing others that he is the way, the truth, and the life that really is life.

No, abiding in Christ is not necessarily an easy task, but my friends I want you to know that Jesus offers us this invitation not to make us feel guilty and not to empower us to work harder. No, Jesus tells his disciples these things so that *his joy may be in them; so that their joy may be complete.* Yes, Jesus has joy and he wants to share. He desires that his disciples know it, share it, and have their joy be complete. Jesus wants them to be filled with joy and so he invites them to "abide in him." Yes, joy is a gift. It is a gift that we do not earn. It is a gift we do not deserve. It is a give we do not have to achieve. Christ offers you and me his joy for free.

Pastor Mary Luti puts it this way:

> And all this time you thought it was about duty, so you've been doing it. You thought it was about making an effort, so you've been making one. You thought it was about becoming a better person and making the world a better place, so you've slogged away. You thought it was about you, about what God wants you to do, about the difference you should be making, about getting the holy job done.

But it was always about joy. The joy of his company. The joy of his grace. The joy of his love for God. The joy of his justice. Even the hard joy of his suffering. It was about being branches of his vine, sheep of his flock, drinking from the living waters of his deep, deep well. It was about doing just and saving work with him, in him, and through him, not for him, like some boss, not to merit a star, and not until you drop.

No, it was for the joy we know when we know him. It was always about joy. It still is.[42]

My friends, take the pulse of your soul. How is the current state of your faith? For Jesus says, I AM: "the bread of life;" "the light of the world;" "the gate" and "the good shepherd;" "the resurrection and the life;" "the way, the truth, and the life;" and "the true vine." That's who he is in his own words. And as we know him, we discover the joy he brings.

It was always about joy. It still is.

Do you believe this?

---

[42] Mary Luti, "For Joy," http://www.ucc.org/daily_devotional_for_joy

Part 3

Called: Flaws and All

And God Said Yes?

1 Samuel 8:4-20

4 Then all the elders of Israel gathered together and came to Samuel at Ramah, 5 and said to him, "You are old and your sons do not follow in your ways; appoint for us, then, a king to govern us, like other nations." 6 But the thing displeased Samuel when they said, "Give us a king to govern us." Samuel prayed to the LORD, 7 and the LORD said to Samuel, "Listen to the voice of the people in all that they say to you; for they have not rejected you, but they have rejected me from being king over them. 8 Just as they have done to me, from the day I brought them up out of Egypt to this day, forsaking me and serving other gods, so also they are doing to you. 9 Now then, listen to their voice; only—you shall solemnly warn them, and show them the ways of the king who shall reign over them."

10 So Samuel reported all the words of the LORD to the people who were asking him for a king. 11 He said, "These will be the ways of the king who will reign over you: he will take your sons and appoint them to his chariots and to be his horsemen, and to run before his chariots; 12 and he will appoint for himself commanders of thousands and commanders of fifties, and some to plow his ground and to reap his harvest, and to make his implements of war and the equipment of his chariots. 13 He will take your daughters to be perfumers and cooks and bakers. 14 He will take the best of your fields and vineyards and olive orchards and give them to his courtiers. 15 He will take one-tenth of your grain and of your vineyards and give it to his officers and his courtiers. 16 He will take your male and female slaves, and the best of your cattle and donkeys, and put them to his work. 17 He will take one-tenth of your flocks, and you shall be his slaves. 18 And in that day you will cry out because of your king, whom you have chosen for yourselves; but the LORD will not answer you in that day."

19 But the people refused to listen to the voice of Samuel; they said, "No! But we are determined to have a king over us, 20 so that we also may be like other nations, and that our king may govern us and go out before us and fight our battles."

"If all of your friends were jumping off a bridge, would you jump too?" Did your mother or father ever ask you that question?

Obviously an attempt to persuade you to rethink a potentially bad idea, right?

So if that question ever came your way (and I am sure it did not due to the high morals and great wisdom you exhibited as a teenager), but if it did I hope you never replied, "Well, it depends on how high the bridge is," or "Is there water underneath this bridge and how deep?" "What about if the bridge is on fire or we are all being chased by a grizzly bear?" Equally unacceptable would be, "Maybe if I had a bungee cord," or "Of course not, we only *all* jump off bridges on Thursdays." Yes, kids I do not recommend any of those responses if this particular question comes your way from a well-meaning but exasperated parent, pastor, or other adult.

But I do need to let you in on a little secret. Writer Chris Guillebeau puts it this way:

> Then, you grow up and suddenly the tables are turned. People start expecting you to behave exactly as they do. If you don't conform to their expectations, some of them get confused or even irritated.
>
> It's almost as if they are asking: "Hey, everyone else is jumping off the bridge. Why aren't you?"
>
> The irony of this is lost on everyone who is busy lining up to take the leap. The logic shifts from independent thinking to groupthink. *If everyone else is doing it, it must be right.*[43]

My friends I ask you to ponder that this morning because I think it is easy to read this text and immediately side with Samuel. After all, two hundred and forty two years ago, we Americans told the world what we think of kings, right? No use for them – democracy and a republic are the way to go. Of course Samuel is right. The people want a king so that "they can be like all the other nations." Yes, everyone else is doing it, but it is like jumping off a bridge. Having a

---

[43] Chris Guillebeau, "A Short Note on Bridge Jumping," https://chrisguillebeau.com/a-short-note-on-bridge-jumping/

king in Isreal is like the peer pressure argument of early Middle Eastern nation building, right? Just say no.

But then why does God say yes?

Because God has been pretty consistent starting with the call to Abraham back in Genesis, chapter 12:

> Go from your country and your kindred and your father's house to the land that I will show you. I will make of you a great nation, and I will bless you, and make your name great, so that you will be a blessing. I will bless those who bless you, and the one who curses you I will curse; and in you all the families of the earth shall be blessed.[44]

Yes, the idea from the beginning for these people God has called, is that they shall be a blessing to all the other families and nations of the earth.

Generations later, after years of slavery in Egypt, God rescues the people and brings them through the wilderness of Sinai with a 40 year-long Exodus journey. As they prepare to finally enter the Promised Land, Moses tells the people:

> If you will only obey the LORD your God, by diligently observing all his commandments that I am commanding you today, the LORD your God will set you high above all the nations of the earth; all these blessings shall come upon you and overtake you, if you obey the LORD your God.[45]

If they will only obey the Lord their God, they will be lifted high above all the nations of the earth. Everyone will be looking to Israel for wisdom and guidance and inspiration about how a nation might best be governed. Yes, God is clear that if all is well; if the people of Israel are who they are called to be; then all the nations of the earth

---

[44] Genesis 12:1-3
[45] Deuteronomy 28:1-2

will seek to be like <u>them</u>! And yet, here the elders come and ask for a king "so that we might be like all the other nations."

And God says yes?

Again, it is easy for us to judge the people of Israel with this request. We like to think that the question of our mothers and fathers about not jumping off a bridge with all of our friends somehow still guides our actions today. But the power of "groupthink" is so strong. If everyone else is doing it, it must be right. Whether it is the kind of house we buy or the neighborhood we "have" to live in. Whether we have to send our kids to private schools or public schools. Whether we rent our houses for Masters or not. Whether we like or forward that off-color joke or questionable picture on Facebook. Whether we support this political candidate or that one. Whether we spend our weekends in the mountains or at the beach. It does not matter if we are called to it, if it matches our gifts or interests, or if it is going to stretch us too far financially. No, if everybody is doing it, it must be right.

We face the same temptation as the church. Sometimes we call it "parking lot theology." We look around our city and find whichever church has the fullest parking lot. People are going to that church so they must be doing something right. Therefore, we should do the same thing. Whether it is a new worship style or type of music; a different kind of preaching; a particular moral or political stance; a new building for children or youth or senior adults; adding small groups or large groups or mission trips or local partnerships. Whatever that church is doing, we need to do it too because we want our parking lot to be full just like all the other churches. It does not matter if we are called to it, if it matches our gifts or interests, or if it is going to stretch us too far financially. If everybody is doing it, it must be right.

And not just our church here in Augusta, but the church in general struggles with this temptation. German theologian and martyr Dietrich Bonhoeffer once wrote:

Christianity stands or falls with its revolutionary protest against violence, arbitrariness, and pride of power, and with its plea for the weak. Christians are doing too little to make these points clear rather than too much. Christendom adjusts itself far too easily to the worship of power. Christians should give more offense, shock the world far more, than they are doing now. Christians should take a stronger stand in favor of the weak rather than considering first the possible right of the strong.[46]

It is so easy for the church, just as it was for Israel so many years ago, to put its faith in the nation instead of in the Lord, to serve the interests of the powerful instead of the weak.

And God says yes?

The people of Israel want a king. They want to be like other nations. God correctly recognizes that this behavior is nothing new. The people have been seeking after idols and placing their trust in other gods ever since God brought them up out of Egypt. And we have not changed a bit. We are willing to find our guidance in our political leaders rather than in God. We are willing to put our trust in the market as opposed to the Lord. After all, everyone else is doing it. Even when Samuel warns the people, even when we hear today, that we are denying our call to be a light to the nations, that we are treating our citizens and our guests worse than our enemies, that we are making ourselves slaves to our leaders, the people say, "Sure, let's do it."

And God says yes.

From the beginning it has been pretty clear: The people of Israel are called to trust in the Lord, but they fail to do so. They want a king to fight their battles for them, so they are willing to put their trust in a king instead of God. Always a bad idea.

---

[46] Dietrich Bonhoeffer, in a Sermon on *II Corinthians 12:9*,
http://www.godandculture.com/blog/bonhoeffer-on-christians-and-the-worship-of-power

But they are not alone in this call to trust in the Lord. Samuel knows that asking for a king is a horrible idea. It is a denial of the people's fundamental identity and a return to slavery. Samuel must have been shocked when God said, "Listen to the voice of the people and give them a king." So, Samuel presents about the possibly worse case senario of what it will be like to have a king and still both the people and God are steadfast. They want a king and God says give them one. So the real challenge in this text is that Samuel must now live into his own convinctions. *He too must trust and obey the Lord.*

For what Samuel and we so often forget is that God has a larger view of history than we do.

Perhaps God says yes because God knows that while the first king, Saul, will be a disaster, that a king after God's own heart, David, will follow.

Perhaps God says yes because God knows that while the kings following David will lead to destruction and exile and despair, there will one day be a king born in the city of David, who will save us all from our sins. As author Doug Bratt writes:

> Of course, God's will alone is good. God knew what was best for Israel, just as God's knows what's best for all of God's adopted sons and daughters. God knew that it would be best for Israel if he alone were her king. Yet God told Samuel to give Israel the king she wanted anyway.
>
> Those kings, of course, help lead Israel's downhill charge toward ungodliness that ends up in her near-obliteration. However, the Lord graciously used even Israel's deeply flawed and disobedient desire for a monarch to work out the Lord's own will. After all, who turns out to be not just Israel's, but also the whole world's King? Jesus Christ ... a great, great, great grandson of one of Israel's kings, David.[47]

---

[47] Doug Bratt, "Old Testament Lectionary – 1 Samuel 8:4-11, (12-15), 16-20, (11:14-15)," http://cep.calvinseminary.edu/sermon-starters/proper-5b-2/?type=old_testament_lectionary

My friends, do not jump off that bridge. It is always a bad idea. Trust in the Lord. For if we obey the Lord, if we are a light to the nations, if we are a church embracing our unique and wonderful call for this time and this place, then all of Augusta will be blessed through us.

And yet, even when we fall short, even when we fail, even when we call for a king of our own, we still must trust in the Lord. For even our greatest failures, might be the opportunity for God's greatest triumph.

With God's Help
1 Samuel 17:31-50

³¹ When the words that David spoke were heard, they repeated them before Saul; and he sent for him. ³² David said to Saul, "Let no one's heart fail because of him; your servant will go and fight with this Philistine." ³³ Saul said to David, "You are not able to go against this Philistine to fight with him; for you are just a boy, and he has been a warrior from his youth." ³⁴ But David said to Saul, "Your servant used to keep sheep for his father; and whenever a lion or a bear came, and took a lamb from the flock, ³⁵ I went after it and struck it down, rescuing the lamb from its mouth; and if it turned against me, I would catch it by the jaw, strike it down, and kill it. ³⁶ Your servant has killed both lions and bears; and this uncircumcised Philistine shall be like one of them, since he has defied the armies of the living God." ³⁷ David said, "The LORD, who saved me from the paw of the lion and from the paw of the bear, will save me from the hand of this Philistine." So Saul said to David, "Go, and may the LORD be with you!"

³⁸ Saul clothed David with his armor; he put a bronze helmet on his head and clothed him with a coat of mail. ³⁹ David strapped Saul's sword over the armor, and he tried in vain to walk, for he was not used to them. Then David said to Saul, "I cannot walk with these; for I am not used to them." So David removed them. ⁴⁰ Then he took his staff in his hand, and chose five smooth stones from the wadi, and put them in his shepherd's bag, in the pouch; his sling was in his hand, and he drew near to the Philistine.

⁴¹ The Philistine came on and drew near to David, with his shield-bearer in front of him. ⁴² When the Philistine looked and saw David, he disdained him, for he was only a youth, ruddy and handsome in appearance. ⁴³ The Philistine said to David, "Am I a dog, that you come to me with sticks?" And the Philistine cursed David by his gods. ⁴⁴ The Philistine said to David, "Come to me, and I will give your flesh to the birds of the air and to the wild animals of the field." ⁴⁵ But David said to the Philistine, "You come to me with sword and spear and javelin; but I come to you in the name of the LORD of hosts, the God of the armies of Israel, whom you have defied. ⁴⁶ This very day the LORD will deliver you into my hand, and I will strike you down and cut off your head; and I will give the dead bodies of the Philistine army this very day to the birds of the air and to the wild animals of the earth, so that all the earth may know that there is a God in Israel, ⁴⁷ and that all this assembly may know that the LORD does not save by sword and spear; for the battle is the LORD's and he will give you into our hand."

⁴⁸ When the Philistine drew nearer to meet David, David ran quickly toward the battle line to meet the Philistine. ⁴⁹ David put his hand in his bag, took out a stone, slung it, and struck the Philistine on his forehead; the stone sank into his forehead, and he fell face down on the ground.

⁵⁰ So David prevailed over the Philistine with a sling and a stone, striking down the Philistine and killing him; there was no sword in David's hand.

This is the ultimate dramatic story, isn't it? A challenge is issued, a crowd cowers in fear, and then finally one stands up to defend his people's honor. Not a warrior, but a boy. Not armed to the teeth, but a shepherd with a sling and five smooth stones. Can the underdog emerge triumphant – of course he will because this story has become iconic.

People of all ages love this story, but especially children. When my boys were small, we loved to watch the Veggie Tales version of David and Goliath. I think I loved that version as much or even more than they did. For those who might not remember, Veggie Tales faithfully depicted biblical stories with animated talking vegetables as the main characters. In this case, a little asparagus named Dave confronts a quite ugly and mean Giant Pickle. The stone flies from the slingshot and knocks the giant on his head. The pickle falls causing a terrible crash. The Israelite vegetables cheer, the Philistine French peas run away, and Dave the asparagus rides off on a sheep singing, "With God's help, little guys can do big things too."

I mention that Veggie Tales version this morning because that song reminds us of something we adults often miss in this story. Yes, "*With God's help*, little guys can do big things too." When we tell this story, we tend to focus on the little guy's courage or superior military tactics. This story becomes a metaphor for athletic contests in which heart and scrap and bravery triumph over apparent talent and strength. Popular journalist and writer Malcolm Gladwell has even written a book called, "David and Goliath," in which he explores: "What happens when ordinary people confront giants ... [or] powerful opponents of all kinds – from armies and mighty warriors to disability, misfortune, and oppression."[48]

Now, I will admit Gladwell has written a good book, but as inspirational as the stories that we adults tell about underdogs overcoming seemingly unsurmountable odds, we tend to lose the most important aspect of the actual biblical story: *With God's help.* And when we miss God's place in the story, we find ourselves trapped with one of the four other responses to the crisis.

First, on one side of the valley we find the Philistines. The Philistines are the constant threat to Israel during these early days of monarchy. The Philistines are known for their advances in technology and have a near monopoly on the production of iron.[49] Goliath's armor and weapons indicate this superiority – a bronze helmet, a coat of mail, a javelin, and a massive spear made of iron. All of this technology makes the Philistines arrogant and overconfident. If there is a battle to be fought, surely, we will win ... have you ever heard that before?

Emerging from the arrogance of the Philistines' technology and military weaponry is the second option – the ultimate bully Goliath. He stands six cubits and a span – nearly 7 feet tall. He is so well armed that he needs someone else to carry his shield. He taunts the Israelites: "Choose a man for yourselves and let him come down to me. If he is able to fight with me and kill me, then we will be your servants; but if I prevail against him and kill him, then you shall be our servants and serve us." You only make that kind of challenge if you are confident that you are going to win. The arrogance of the bully draws every eye in the valley – both Philistines and Israelites - to himself. He dominates everything. Have you ever heard that before?

Looking at the giant and hearing his insults, the people of Israel are filled with fear. No one accepts Goliath's challenge. Day after day the bully shouts his insults. The people see him and hear him, but

---

[48] Malcolm Gladwell, *David and Goliath*, 5.
[49] 1 Samuel 13:19-22

fear paralyzes them. Circle the wagons, keep everyone safe, don't let anyone stand out, maintain the status quo, and certainly do not confront the bully because he might turn on you. Have you ever heard that before?

Yes, the arrogant, the bully, the fearful. There is one more. When the people of Israel first called out for a king, they "wanted to be like the other nations" and to have a king "who would lead them into battle."[50] That's exactly the king they found in Saul. He stood a head taller than anyone else in Israel. There was "none like him among all the people."[51] Saul had led them into battle and for a while he had been quite skilled at it. Even in our text for today, we find that Saul has his own complete set of armor – bronze helmet, coat of mail, and a sword. Saul is the champion of Israel. His power and courage are found in his height, his strength, and his weapons.

But now he has encountered one who is taller, stronger, and better armed. He does not know what to do. When David appears and declares that he will fight Goliath, Saul initially protests. When convinced that David will not be deterred, Saul tries his very best to help. In fact, he helps the only way he knew how: pile on the armor, protect yourself, and get a weapon with proven effectiveness. Saul allows Goliath to set the terms of the battle. Goliath has asked for hand to hand combat, so Saul tries to prepare David for it. He cannot see another way. He keeps doing what he has always done and hopes for different results. Have you ever heard that before?

So, these are the four options that David encounters when he enters the valley with provisions for his brothers. One arrogant army and one fearful army. A bully casting insults and a supposed champion stuck in an old paradigm. All eyes on Goliath. All conversation about Goliath. As Presbyterian pastor and writer Eugene Peterson says:

> David entered the valley with a God–dominated, not a Goliath dominated imagination … He couldn't believe what he was seeing and hearing – Goliath terror, Goliath phobia. It was an epidemic worse than cholera, everyone down with

---

[50] 1 Samuel 8:5 and 20
[51] 1 Samuel 10:23 and 24

Goliath sickness, a terrible disease of spirit that had Saul and his entire army incapacitated.[52]

David sees another way. Yes, we tell this story as the triumph of David over Goliath. But David says this is a story about God.

In a world of traditional power, where might makes right, David doesn't have a chance. But David doesn't see the world in those terms, in which power is held *only* by human hands, wits, and weapons. No, David sees a world where there's power in a name, the name YHWH – the God who delivers.

For YHWH had seen the people's suffering and heard their cry in Egypt, so he delivered them from their slavery. YHWH had heard the people's cry as they entered the Promised Land, so he delivered them from the Canaanites. When the Philistines had attacked before and the people cried out, YHWH had raised up judges to deliver them. This is the history of the people of Israel: their God delivers if only the people will call out and trust in Him.

Before Saul, before Goliath, David calls on YHWH by name. He seems to be the only one in the whole valley who remembers that there is a God in Israel because he has personal experience with this God. "The Lord who saved me from the paw of the lion and from the paw of the bear will save me from the hand of this Philistine," is what David tells Saul. In the face of Goliath's threats and curses, David responds, "This very day the Lord will deliver you into my hand ... so that all the earth may know that there is a God in Israel, and that all this assembly may know that the Lord does not save by sword and spear; for the battle is the Lord's and he will give you into our hand."

On those terms, on those theological terms, both Saul and Goliath with their conventional power world view are severely overmatched. Both the arrogance of the Philistine army and the paralyzing fear of the Israelite army fall away. David stakes his life on the power of YHWH. The battle is brief, only two verses after 47 verses of

---

[52] Eugene Peterson, *Leap Over a Wall*, 40.

buildup. *With God's help* David emerges victorious. Now there can be no doubt that there is a God in Israel, a living God, a God who delivers not with sword and spear, but in God's inscrutable ways.

My friends in the midst of this crazy world we so often fall into one of the other four options when confronted with a crisis. We are arrogant in our weapons, technology, and abilities. We let the bullies of this world dominate the public square and set the agenda. We are paralyzed by fear and despair. We keep trying the same things with no different results.

We are called to live another way — a way of a God-dominated consciousness, a way of faith and courage that calls forth our very best gifts from us. Will people look at you and at me and at us and say, "Surely there is a God with them?"

When He Began to Reign
2 Samuel 5:1-10

¹Then all the tribes of Israel came to David at Hebron, and said, "Look, we are your bone and flesh. ²For some time, while Saul was king over us, it was you who led out Israel and brought it in. The LORD said to you: It is you who shall be shepherd of my people Israel, you who shall be ruler over Israel." ³So all the elders of Israel came to the king at Hebron; and King David made a covenant with them at Hebron before the LORD, and they anointed David king over Israel. ⁴David was thirty years old when he began to reign, and he reigned forty years. ⁵At Hebron he reigned over Judah seven years and six months; and at Jerusalem he reigned over all Israel and Judah thirty-three years.

⁶The king and his men marched to Jerusalem against the Jebusites, the inhabitants of the land, who said to David, "You will not come in here, even the blind and the lame will turn you back"—thinking, "David cannot come in here." ⁷Nevertheless David took the stronghold of Zion, which is now the city of David. ⁸David had said on that day, "Whoever would strike down the Jebusites, let him get up the water shaft to attack the lame and the blind, those whom David hates." Therefore it is said, "The blind and the lame shall not come into the house." ⁹David occupied the stronghold, and named it the city of David. David built the city all around from the Millo inward. ¹⁰And David became greater and greater, for the LORD, the God of hosts, was with him.

The first church I served after graduating from seminary was the Salem/Pageland Presbyterian Church in Pageland, SC. We moved to the area about two weeks before my ordination. I wanted to be able to hit the ground running when I actually started serving, so I asked the clerk of session if we could meet to have lunch. She was happy to do it and suggested that we meet at Eddie's Pit Stop.

I discovered that Eddie's Pit Stop was a small one-man grill on Route 9 just outside of Pageland. Arriving a bit early, I went in to wait. Opening the door, as my eyes adjusted to the dimmer light, I heard, "Well, hello Reverend." Thinking I might have an opportunity to meet one of my new pastoral colleagues, I turned around to see who else might have come in behind me. Not seeing anyone, I looked at the half a dozen or so tables to see if someone just looked like a pastor. It is always dangerous to make assumptions based on appearance, but it did not appear to me that there were any pastors in Eddie's Pit Stop that day. So, I kept walking and heard again, "Hello, Reverend." I followed the voice to the man standing and smiling behind the grill. It was only then that I realized there was a "Reverend" in Eddie's Pit Stop - me! Turns out Eddie was a member of the church. He recognized me from my picture in the Pastor Nominating Committee report.

Yes, that was first time I remember someone I did not expect, or even yet know, call me by this title, identifying me as: "Reverend." It caught me off guard. I realized that something had changed.

That became even more evident just a few weeks later when I knelt at the front of the sanctuary of the Summersville Presbyterian Church. We had moved to Summersville on the day I started sixth grade. My family joined the church later that fall. I had stood in front of that church on the day I made my public profession of faith. I sang in the choir from time to time when I was in high school. I had even climbed into the pulpit every year on Youth Sunday, a little nervous but also a bit arrogant to believe that as a teenager I could preach the Word of God! Yes, that congregation had loved me and prayed for me while I was student at Davidson College and Union Presbyterian Seminary. That church and these people felt like home.

And yet, as I knelt there before them for the prayer of ordination, the hands of the commission from the Presbytery of West Virginia resting on my head and shoulders, I suddenly felt the weight of it all. Something significant was happening. This calling from God to serve as a pastor had a gravitas, a heaviness, to it that I had not expected. As I knelt there those hands seemed so heavy on my head and on my shoulders.

Then, after the "Amen" of the prayer, those same hands helped me to stand. They literally lifted me up and I knew I was not in this calling alone. But something had changed. I had knelt down as a recent seminary graduate. When I stood I was a Minster of Word and Sacrament in the Presbyterian Church (USA). In a real and yet somehow mysterious way, I suddenly felt I could now answer the next time Eddie said, "Hello, Reverend," when I walked into the Pit Stop. What happened after I answered, well that was yet to be seen.

Something like all of that is going on in our text for today. When the elders of Israel come to Hebron to see David something real and yet mysterious is happening. David had been anointed by Samuel many years ago. Do you remember how God sends Samuel to Bethlehem to anoint one of the sons of Jesse as the next king of Israel? Samuel sees seven young men before him; God rejects them all. But there is one more: the youngest. He is out in the fields keeping the sheep. So, they send for this shepherd boy and when he arrives Samuel anoints him as king.

It is not with the weapons of a heavily armed warrior, but with a shepherd's sling and a stone that this shepherd boy will defeat the Philistine giant Goliath. As he grows he will lead the people of Israel in battle; he will dodge the attempts King Saul makes on his life; he will hide out in the wilderness; he will spare the life of the king; and he will lead his own tribe. Through it all, David trusts in the Lord. He finds his perseverance and strength not in himself, but in YHWH – the God who delivers. He is now a little taller, a little older, but he still carries the simple faith in God he had as that shepherd boy.

Yes, when the elders of Israel come to Hebron to see David something real and yet mysterious is happening. "Look, we are your bone and flesh. For some time, while Saul was king over us, it was you who led out Israel and brought it in. The LORD said to you: It is you who shall be shepherd of my people Israel, you who shall be [prince] over Israel." It is like they are saying, "David, you know that we are all family here. Even when Saul was king, you were the real leader of our armies. So, remember what the Lord said to you."

You shall be our *shepherd*. Yes, the shepherd is the model leader in Israel. Think of the words of Psalm 23, "The Lord is my shepherd, I shall not want." The shepherd provides green pastures, and still waters, right paths, protection in the darkest valley, and feast in the presence of enemies. The shepherd cares for and protects the sheep. That is what the leader of Israel should do.

When later kings fail miserably at this task, the prophets will criticize them for eating the fat and clothing themselves while ignoring the sheep. For example, Ezekiel declares:

> You have not strengthened the weak, you have not healed the sick, you have not bound up the injured, you have not brought back the strayed, you have not sought the lost, but with force and harshness you have ruled them.[53]

The leader of Israel is to be a good shepherd. And that vision begins with David, the shepherd boy who becomes the shepherd king.

But wait, not yet a shepherd "king." At least that is not what the rulers of Israel request. The prophet Samuel had warned them about kings. Their recent experience with Saul confirmed the pitfalls that kings bring. The word in Hebrew for king is *melek* and it is used several places in this text, but not in the elders' request. No, they use the word, *nagid*, which literally means "prince." They remember in this moment that YHWH is king of Israel and the earthly shepherd of the people is God's prince. There is a limit to monarchial power in Israel marked by the covenant between God, the prince, and the people.

Yes, something real and yet mysterious is happening when the elders of Israel come to Hebron to see David. The shepherd boy becomes the shepherd of Israel. The youngest son of Jesse becomes the prince over all the people. And David makes a covenant with the all the elders of Israel at Hebron before the Lord, and they anointed David "king."

I thought he was supposed to be the prince?

But they anoint David "king" over Israel and something changes in him. From this point on in this story, there appears to be a struggle within David. Is he the shepherd caring for his sheep or is he the king consolidating power? Is he the shepherd laying down his life or is he the king taking life for his own gain? Is he the shepherd

---

[53] Ezekiel 34:4

rescuing the weak or is he the king throwing out all who cannot produce something of value to him?

Yes, David is called "king" and we do not have to wait long to see what happens next.

Immediately after his anointing, David seeks to find a political capital for his reign. He chooses Jerusalem, the city of the Jebusites; a city on the border between the territory of the tribe of Judah and the territory occupied by the northern tribes. The city was thought to be so well fortified, so unconquerable, that the Jebusites taunt David that even the blind and the lame could defend it.

And yet, what David says in response is absolutely horrifying: "Whoever would strike down the Jebusites, let him get up the water shaft to attack the lame and the blind, those whom David hates." Therefore, it is said, "The blind and the lame shall not come into the house." These are not the words of a good shepherd. These are the words of angry and impulsive king. Yes, something has changed in David – and not for the better.

My friends, I ask you this morning to consider what you are called. It might not be as stark as being called "Reverend" for the first time in public. It might not come with the heavy hands of ordination or anointing as shepherd and prince by the elders of Israel. But, my friends God's call to you is still just as sure. You were once the child of your parents, but they handed you over to a pastor to be baptized. After the water was poured over your head, the pastor handed you back and you were now called "child of God."

That is who you are. That is your real name. For you are called to follow not King David, but the one who came to Jerusalem giving sight to the blind and new strength to the legs of the lame. The one who was crowned not on a throne in a palace but who found his throne on a cross just outside the walls of the city of David.

Yes, something real and yet mysterious has happened to you. Will you answer when Jesus calls you by name? What happens after that, remains to be seen.

Dancing before the Lord
2 Samuel 6:1-15

¹ David again gathered all the chosen men of Israel, thirty thousand. ² David and all the people with him set out and went from Baale-judah, to bring up from there the ark of God, which is called by the name of the LORD of hosts who is enthroned on the cherubim. ³ They carried the ark of God on a new cart, and brought it out of the house of Abinadab, which was on the hill. Uzzah and Ahio, the sons of Abinadab, were driving the new cart ⁴ with the ark of God; and Ahio went in front of the ark. ⁵ David and all the house of Israel were dancing before the LORD with all their might, with songs and lyres and harps and tambourines and castanets and cymbals.

⁶ When they came to the threshing floor of Nacon, Uzzah reached out his hand to the ark of God and took hold of it, for the oxen shook it. ⁷ The anger of the LORD was kindled against Uzzah; and God struck him there because he reached out his hand to the ark; and he died there beside the ark of God. ⁸ David was angry because the LORD had burst forth with an outburst upon Uzzah; so that place is called Perez-uzzah, to this day. ⁹ David was afraid of the LORD that day; he said, "How can the ark of the LORD come into my care?" ¹⁰ So David was unwilling to take the ark of the LORD into his care in the city of David; instead David took it to the house of Obed-edom the Gittite. ¹¹ The ark of the LORD remained in the house of Obed-edom the Gittite three months; and the LORD blessed Obed-edom and all his household.

¹² It was told King David, "The LORD has blessed the household of Obed-edom and all that belongs to him, because of the ark of God." So David went and brought up the ark of God from the house of Obed-edom to the city of David with rejoicing; ¹³ and when those who bore the ark of the LORD had gone six paces, he sacrificed an ox and a fatling. ¹⁴ David danced before the LORD with all his might; David was girded with a linen ephod. ¹⁵ So David and all the house of Israel brought up the ark of the LORD with shouting, and with the sound of the trumpet.

I think it is important to acknowledge, right up front this morning, that we face some pretty stiff competition today with our 10:30 AM worship service. It is not just that it is a beautiful, although slightly warm, day in the middle of summer vacation season. It is not even that there are hundreds of other churches, just in Augusta, holding worship services at this same time today. No, our competition is much larger than that.

For just a few minutes ago, at 11:00 AM Eastern Daylight Time, the final match in the world's largest sporting event kicked off. Over the last month the FIFA World Cup has been played in Russia and today is the tournament's final match: France vs. Croatia. Despite the fact that both are fairly small nations in terms of population, the international appeal of soccer means that more than 1 billion people, yes more than 1 billion (with a B) people are expected to watch the match today.

Many around the world are watching the match on their mobile device. Perhaps some of you are following the game that way even while you sit here at church! (If so, don't tell me the score as I'm going to try to catch it all later on replay). As the games have been played during the day here in the States due to the time difference, I have mainly kept up with the scores over the internet. However, in the games I was able to watch live I was fascinated by not only the coverage of the games, but also of the huge outdoor watch parties in the nations engaged in a particular match. An entire public square packed with people, eyes lifted to massive screens. Suddenly you can see them all collectively hold their breath, rise up on their toes, and then with one voice erupting with shouts of elation and joy as a goal is scored. Everyone is hugging everyone else. Hands in the air, cheers and celebration, together as one. It is truly impressive to behold.

In our text for today we find a similar whole community collective celebration. To understand what is going on, I think we first need to take a step back into the history of Israel. The Israelites had constructed the ark during their Exodus journey from Egypt to Canaan. At Mt. Sinai God gave Moses specific instructions on how to construct the ark, what it was to look like, and what it was to contain.[54] It was made by the finest craftsman in Israel and overlaid with pure gold. Its top was shaped with cherubim whose wings formed a mercy seat or throne for God himself to sit upon. Inside

---

[54] Exodus 25

were the original stone tablets on which the Ten Commandments had been written and a sample of the manna eaten by the Israelites on their Exodus journey. As you can see, for these wandering, tribal descendants of Jacob, during the Exodus the ark was designed to be a physical manifestation of God's presence with the people.

Therefore, wherever the ark went great holiness surrounded it. If the Israelites took the ark into battle, they emerged victorious. One time when the ark fell into the hands of the Philistines, a large statue of the enemy's god was found lying face down before the ark the next morning. Whenever the ark rested in the ceremonial tent known as the "tabernacle," the cloud of God's presence would rest on that place. Once when approximately seventy men looked inside the ark, the Lord struck them dead. Wherever the ark was housed and was treated with respect, blessing came upon that house. Yes, the ark was the ultimate religious object.

That blessing, holiness, and power was exactly what David was looking for when he went to get the ark from the house of Abinadab. It had been twenty years since anyone had even thought about the ark.[55] King Saul and his administration never went looking for it or even mentioned the ark. It is almost as if the ark was a symbol of God's presence from days gone by. Now that there was a king, why did they need a holy box?

But David knew that for his administration and rule to succeed where Saul's had failed, he needed some present symbol of the divine anointing he had received as a child, some outward sign that he was God's chosen one. So David goes to get the ark. He seems to want it for the ways it will help him. Thus, David leads the parade, bringing the power, presence, and holiness of God to *his* house, to *his* city, to stand behind *his* throne.

But something happens on the road to Jerusalem. This triumphant military procession of the Ark to its new home in David's political capital becomes a nationwide World Cup watch party. David, his 30,000 men, and it appears the entire nation of Israel are dancing

---

[55] 1 Samuel 7:2

before the LORD with all their might, with songs and lyres and harps and tambourines and castanets (who knew those were in the bible?) and cymbals. This was not just a little foot tapping or the obligatory sway with the music. It was more like the Social, Inc. Spring Formal with thousands of teenagers filling every inch of the floor of the James Brown Arena, all dancing together. And King David is leading them all, dancing before the Lord with all his might. The Hebrew word captures the essence of this. It says that David danced with all his *YAZ*. Isn't that a great word, with all his *YAZ* – with every ounce of strength and might that he had within him. Everything deep down within him is unleashed as he whirls and twirls before the Lord. David and all the people of Israel are swept away by this parade of the ark.

But then it all stops. Uzzah is lying dead on the floor!

No matter how many times I read this story, I always have a "What?" moment about half way through. Yes, we seem to be reading a nice story of a community parade and giant party, with great pomp and circumstance, as David brings the Ark of the Covenant to Jerusalem. But then, Uzzah touches the ark with his hand to steady it, and God strikes him dead! What? Someone who appears to be caring for the ark is lying dead in the street. Immediately, the parade and party comes to a halt.

Just as it does for us as readers, Uzzah's death stops David in his tracks. He is angry with the Lord for striking Uzzah. Why would God do such a thing, especially when Uzzah was only trying to help? The text leaves that question unanswered and so must we.

But that mystery makes David very afraid. He has just witnessed firsthand the power and holiness of the ark. Up to this point the ark had been a symbol of power, but not really powerful itself. It told the story of holiness in the desert, but it was not really holy itself. This had been a parade about our great new king David and all the people are swept up in <u>*David's*</u> glory. But that parade is over. The holiness and power of God are upfront and present! David is afraid of the Lord and the ark as both have holiness and power beyond his imagination and, more importantly, beyond his control.

There are times, I think, that just like David, we get carried away in the hubbub and excitement of "us," in our own importance and power. In those times we like our God to be very small, to be a symbol we can show ourselves and others of how great we are and how righteous our ideas and actions are. We domesticate God into someone who just confirms what we are and what we think and know. God becomes useful to us, making us comfortable and safe. We think that God serves _us_, instead of you and I each serving God.

The death of Uzzah shows us that God is so much bigger than that. God is so much more powerful, so much more holy, than we could ever imagine. Even with the very best of intentions, an individual or a community that forgets God's holiness and power stands at great risk. Not only do we lose the wonder and grandeur of God when our eyes are looking only at ourselves, but our God refuses to be so limited and used! We might even say that even with the holiness and power of the ark, God refuses to be put only in that box!

So, my friends, wherever your journey in life takes you, and whatever watch parties you find yourselves in, I pray that you will not be dragging a little god in a box behind you to justify your trip. Because if our God becomes too small, then God will only do small things, like make us feel good about our sinful selves.

But our God is big, awesome, and holy and our God is transforming this world of sin through Jesus Christ. In our journey of faith and life we need a little healthy fear of the Lord, a little reverence and awe and wonder at God's holiness and power. When David remembers that, the parade continues and once again we find the king and all the people dancing before the Lord with all their YAZ, with all their might. May that be the case for us today at Reid Memorial Presbyterian Church as together with hearts, and minds, and one voice all the people say: "Amen!"

God's House

2 Samuel 7:1-14a

¹Now when the king was settled in his house, and the LORD had given him rest from all his enemies around him, ² the king said to the prophet Nathan, "See now, I am living in a house of cedar, but the ark of God stays in a tent." ³ Nathan said to the king, "Go, do all that you have in mind; for the LORD is with you."

⁴ But that same night the word of the LORD came to Nathan: ⁵ Go and tell my servant David: Thus says the LORD: Are you the one to build me a house to live in? ⁶ I have not lived in a house since the day I brought up the people of Israel from Egypt to this day, but I have been moving about in a tent and a tabernacle. ⁷ Wherever I have moved about among all the people of Israel, did I ever speak a word with any of the tribal leaders of Israel, whom I commanded to shepherd my people Israel, saying, "Why have you not built me a house of cedar?" ⁸ Now therefore thus you shall say to my servant David: Thus says the LORD of hosts: I took you from the pasture, from following the sheep to be prince over my people Israel; ⁹ and I have been with you wherever you went, and have cut off all your enemies from before you; and I will make for you a great name, like the name of the great ones of the earth. ¹⁰ And I will appoint a place for my people Israel and will plant them, so that they may live in their own place, and be disturbed no more; and evildoers shall afflict them no more, as formerly, ¹¹ from the time that I appointed judges over my people Israel; and I will give you rest from all your enemies. Moreover, the LORD declares to you that the LORD will make you a house. ¹² When your days are fulfilled and you lie down with your ancestors, I will raise up your offspring after you, who shall come forth from your body, and I will establish his kingdom. ¹³ He shall build a house for my name, and I will establish the throne of his kingdom forever. ¹⁴ I will be a father to him, and he shall be a son to me.

In his book *Leaving North Haven*, Presbyterian minister and author, Michael Lindvall tells fictional stories about the ministry of Rev. David Battles. In one tale, David travels with his family to a neighboring town to watch his clarinet wielding daughter march with her high school band in a Memorial Day parade. They happen to set their folding chairs on the sidewalk by a prominent intersection in front of a large brick building without a sign, but which looked suspiciously like a church. After watching his daughter's band march by David notices an open door in the brick building. A man emerges, sees the pastor's interest, and invites him inside.

David quickly learns from his impromptu tour guide, Carl, that the building indeed was once a church. Which denomination or even the exact name, Carl cannot recall. But the church no longer exists. All Carl knows is that there is a large endowment generating enough money to pay him to clean up around the place and look after the building once a week.

By now, they are standing in the sanctuary. Carl mentions that the plywood-covered windows were at one time filled with beautiful stained glass, telling all the stories of the Bible. But the windows were sold over a decade ago along with the silver communion set and everything else of much value. Carl rattles on, saying he and his wife never came to the church except for the chicken dinners they served each Friday night in the basement. This church was famous for those chicken dinners.

Back in the sunlight, David thanked Carl for the tour. As he waited for his wife to return with the car after picking up their daughter at the end of the parade route, he silently reflected on his visit. How quickly and quietly a church can slip away. Now all that remained was a brick building with plywood windows, no sign, and memories of Friday night chicken dinners.[56]

I wonder if King David had similar reflections as he sat in his cedar planked house thinking about the ark of God in the yard in a tent. Much like the church members in the story who built that now abandoned brick church, David's first inclination is to build God a house that will last. He wants to build a temple so that God might dwell in Jerusalem. This would have been a fairly common idea throughout the Middle East at this time. Canadian biblical scholar Patricia Dutcher-Walls writes,

---

[56] Michael Lindvall, "Thin Wine," *Leaving North Haven*, 156-168.

As with other ancient kings, [David's] next most important task was to build a temple for the God who had established his throne. Generally, temples were built to serve and worship the high god of any nation and in turn functioned to legitimate the king who built them.[57]

And hearing this plan, the prophet Nathan agrees: "Go, do all that you have in mind; for the Lord is with you."

But that night, Nathan gets a different message from the Lord. We might say the building permit has been revoked. For instead of David building a house for God, the Lord is going to build a house for David! This turns out to be a quite significant move in the history of Israel. For kings will no longer be chosen due to their particular charismatic gifts; they will instead come from a single family. Memories of God's moveable presence with the people of Israel during the Exodus are recalled. There is anticipation of the temple that David's son Solomon will build for God in the next generation. And we can even trace the lineage of Jesus as the Messiah, from the House of David, back to this text.

Yes, this is a key text in this narrative of Samuel, Saul, David, and Solomon. But what stands out to me is how God places himself not in a particular plot of land, not in large brick buildings which are too easily abandoned, but in a people. This is the case time and time again in scripture.

At Sinai, God declared, "If you obey my voice and keep my covenant, you shall be my treasured possession out of all the peoples."[58]

Generations after our text for today, the prophet Isaiah announces to King Ahaz, "Look, the young woman is with child and shall bear a son and shall name him Immanuel 'God with us.'"[59]

---

[57] Patricia Dutcher-Walls, "Ninth Sunday After Pentecost, Year B" *The Lectionary Commentary – First Reading*, 203.
[58] Exodus 19:5
[59] Isaiah 7:14

In the New Testament text we read a few minutes ago, the apostle Paul write to the Ephesians,

> So then you are no longer strangers and aliens, but you are citizens with the saints and also members of the household of God, built upon the foundation of the apostles and prophets, with Christ Jesus himself as the cornerstone. In him the whole structure is joined together and grows into a holy temple in the Lord; in whom you also are built together spiritually into a dwelling place for God.[60]

Yes, our God desires to be not in a place, but in a people. So, in our text for today God makes David a promise. When his days are fulfilled and he is laid to rest with his ancestors, his offspring will remain. And that son will have offspring, and more offspring, and so on and so on …each one becoming a living stone in God's house.

Just imagine this house for God for a minute. There are living stones in this house for the apostles and the prophets. Those who gathered in an upper room on the night of Christ's resurrection with the doors locked because they were scared of the authorities. Apostles and prophets to whom Jesus appears, pronouncing a blessing of peace and providing evidence of his resurrection from the dead.[61] Those living stones served as witnesses in Jerusalem, in all Judea and Samaria, and to the ends of the earth.[62]

There are living stones in this house for Perpetua and Felicity, two of a group of Christians martyred in the North African town of Carthage in the year 203. Their deaths are only a few of many for the North African church and are remembered today because of the record they left of their imprisonment and their battles in the arena. Hear a few words recorded after their deaths:

> But Perpetua, that she might have some taste of pain, was pierced between the bones and shrieked out; and when the swordsman's hand wandered still … herself set it upon her

---

[60] Ephesians 2:19-22
[61] John 20:19-22
[62] Acts 1:8

own neck … O most valiant and blessed martyrs! O truly called and elected unto the glory of Our Lord Jesus Christ![63]

Yes, there are living stones in this house for Dominic, Francis of Assisi, and Bonaventure, all medieval clerics and monks who created religious communities to preserve the story and the faith as Europe waded through the Dark Ages. The Dominicans became an order of preaching brothers dedicated to worldwide evangelization and the cure of souls. The Franciscans preached repentance and the kingdom of God, accepting a life of poverty, humility, and simplicity in order to build churches and care for the poor. Bonaventure created a "rule" that continues to influence the practice of Christian spirituality today.[64]

There are living stones in this house for Martin Luther who nailed "Ninety-five Theses" or debating points to the door of the Wittenberg Church. For John Calvin who led the Reformation in Geneva. For John Knox who brought the Presbyterian branch of the church to Scotland. A new age in the story and the faith had dawned.[65]

There are living stones in this house for Francis Makemie who settled on the eastern shore of Virginia in 1683 and began planting Presbyterian churches in the colonies. Makemie played the leading role in organizing the first Presbytery in Philadelphia in 1706 and fought with the colonial governments for the right of dissenting, or non-Church of England, ministers to preach. Lord Cornbury, the governor of New York believed Makemie was an agitator and so forbid him to preach in church buildings. But Makemie publicly disobeyed this order and spent forty-six days in jail. He insisted the governor produce a written law that justified his imprisonment but the governor could not.[66] A living stone of protest and justice even in the early stages of the American colonies.

---

[63] From W.H. Shewring, trans. *The Passion of Perpetua and Felicity.*
[64] Williston Walker, *A History of the Christian Church* 4th edition, 310-322.
[65] Ibid, 425-43.
[66] James Smylie, *A Brief History of the Presbyterians*, 39-43.

There are living stones in this house for a generous Christian gentleman, Robert Alexander Reid who executed his last will and testament in 1869 to establish a trust of land which included the so called "Potato Patch" on Walton Way. In 1878 the trustees began "to erect a brick church placed back from Walton Way at a sufficient distance so as not to obstruct the view from Mr. Reid's residence." Mr. Reid's will also stated, "It is my desire that the church should be named 'The Louise Reid Presbyterian Church.'[67] Apparently the trustees deemed that "Louise" was not a suitable name for a Presbyterian Church and so Reid Memorial was born instead.

My friends can you begin to get a glimpse of what we are a part? Not just a collection of 725 or so souls who gather to worship from time to time inside this brick church today. No, we are part of a grand and glorious collection of living stones in the house of God. You and I are living stones in God's House.

Could King David have even envisioned this house, built upon the foundation of the apostles, the prophets, the martyrs, the monks, the reformers, the missionaries, and our own mothers and fathers, with Jesus Christ as the cornerstone? Not a temple somewhere or a brick building that was once known for its great chicken dinners, but together _we_ are a dwelling place for God.

So, do not let this house quickly and quietly slip away. For we are called, flaws and all, to keep building this house for God. Not with bricks and mortar, but with love. Spend some time this week loving the people. Go visit someone you have not seen in a while; reach out to a new member and go to lunch after church next Sunday; speak to a visitor; spend a little time before or after Sunday School around the coffee pot in the fellowship hall; say you are sorry to someone you have offended; embrace one another.

For that is how we build the kind of house that God desires.

---

[67] Jack Capers and Runa Ware, *The First One Hundred Years in the Life and Work of Reid Memorial Presbyterian Church*, 1.

I Have Sinned

2 Samuel 11:26-12:13

26 When the wife of Uriah heard that her husband was dead, she made lamentation for him. 27 When the mourning was over, David sent and brought her to his house, and she became his wife, and bore him a son.

But the thing that David had done displeased the Lord, 1 and the Lord sent Nathan to David. He came to him, and said to him, "There were two men in a certain city, the one rich and the other poor. 2 The rich man had very many flocks and herds; 3 but the poor man had nothing but one little ewe lamb, which he had bought. He brought it up, and it grew up with him and with his children; it used to eat of his meager fare, and drink from his cup, and lie in his bosom, and it was like a daughter to him. 4 Now there came a traveler to the rich man, and he was loath to take one of his own flock or herd to prepare for the wayfarer who had come to him, but he took the poor man's lamb, and prepared that for the guest who had come to him." 5 Then David's anger was greatly kindled against the man. He said to Nathan, "As the Lord lives, the man who has done this deserves to die; 6 he shall restore the lamb fourfold, because he did this thing, and because he had no pity."

7 Nathan said to David, "You are the man! Thus says the Lord, the God of Israel: I anointed you king over Israel, and I rescued you from the hand of Saul; 8 I gave you your master's house, and your master's wives into your bosom, and gave you the house of Israel and of Judah; and if that had been too little, I would have added as much more. 9 Why have you despised the word of the Lord, to do what is evil in his sight? You have struck down Uriah the Hittite with the sword, and have taken his wife to be your wife, and have killed him with the sword of the Ammonites. 10 Now therefore the sword shall never depart from your house, for you have despised me, and have taken the wife of Uriah the Hittite to be your wife. 11 Thus says the Lord: I will raise up trouble against you from within your own house; and I will take your wives before your eyes, and give them to your neighbor, and he shall lie with your wives in the sight of this very sun. 12 For you did it secretly; but I will do this thing before all Israel, and before the sun." 13 David said to Nathan, "I have sinned against the Lord." Nathan said to David, "Now the Lord has put away your sin; you shall not die.

As children head back to school this week or next, they will once again find themselves in the midst of words. Perhaps the youngest will be learning letters and sounds and experiencing the mystery of how one begins to read. As they grow and learn they will begin to discover the meaning of a word from its context. Others will be listening for the author's voice and intention in a poem or argumentative essay. Even in math one has to answer "word" problems. Yes, learning not just the definition of words, but what they evoke and the power they have is an essential part of education.

For the utterance of a single word has the potential to change the world.

A simple "Yes!" spoken by a woman to a man on one knee holding a ring forever joins their lives and their stories.

"I am pregnant," brings unimaginable joy or, in the case of David and Bathsheba, sets in motion actions leading to murder.

"I need help," uttered into a telephone in the middle of the night causes a mother or father to rise and to go search for a child in trouble.

In the midst of an apathetic crowd, a carefully crafted rallying cry may incite revolutionary action.

A whispered word of truth like, "Me too," may bring down an entire company ... or a kingdom.

In our text for today, the prophet Nathan does most of the talking. He tells the parable, he makes the accusation, and he pronounces the judgment. As the voice of God, Nathan drives this story of lust, coveting, adultery, idolatry, betrayal, cover-up, and murder to its conclusion.

But let us also listen to the words that David speaks. Up to this point David has spoken and people have responded. "Who is that woman?" "Bring her here." "Get me Uriah the Hittite." "Set Uriah in the forefront and then draw back." "Do not let this evil trouble you." That is the kind of speech David is accustomed to making. It is direct and commanding. He is the king after all.

Yet, it is easy to forget, as David did, that all of our words are spoken, indeed our entire lives are lived, in response to God's word. God spoke and creation came into being. At Sinai, God spoke and gave commandments and laws by which this called community must live. God spoke to the prophet Samuel and said, "Anoint this young shepherd boy as king." Through generations of prophets, God spoke to remind Israel that the foundation of the law is justice and mercy.

But so far in this story, David has spoken as if he is the one in charge; the one who gets to speak first. Throughout this summer we have seen that every time David does that it leads to disaster. But finally, David speaks in response to the Word of the Lord. He is no longer the initiator of dialogue. After Nathan finishes his parable about the lamb it is time for David to speak, "As the Lord lives, the man who has done this deserves to die; he shall restore the lamb fourfold, because he did this thing, and because he had no pity." The commanding voice of the king is at it again.

And yet, something is different in these words. Up to this point, David's words have been about gratifying his own wants and desires, about covering up his actions, about declaring that something "evil," like murder, should not trouble his general.

But now these words of kingly judgment betray that somewhere deep inside, David still has a moral sense of justice. Words of the law and the commandments that he learned as a child are still present with him. Torah words or "Instruction" from the Lord about how a community is supposed to live together – David still remembers. David knew that kings should care about justice for the poor, the oppressed, the widows, the orphans, and the strangers. The world may change, a shepherd boy may become king, but the Word of our God stands forever.

God's word is nonnegotiable. Despite our attempts to deny it, we know that. We can try to justify and explain away this action or another, but we know. *We know.*

"The man who has done this deserves to die." With his own words, David condemns himself. Nathan's "You are the man!" is merely a confirmation of what David already knows to be true. The parable has not revealed some new law or instruction from God, it simply holds up a mirror so David can see what he has done and what he has forgotten. In words we use almost every Sunday, David has seen, "how far short he has fallen from all that God has asked him to be and do."

Thus, the luster of David's crown is quite tarnished by the next time he speaks. Again, David speaks only in response to the Word of the Lord. From the mouth of the prophet, David has heard words of judgment: his kingdom will know war; his own family will be in turmoil; and his wives will be taken and given to another. Severe, but not entirely unexpected. If you send someone to be killed in battle, the violence will not end there. If you commit adultery, your family will suffer. If you break relationship, you will lose something. Sin has consequences.

Hearing all this, David utters two words in Hebrew that come out as six in English, "I have sinned against the Lord." We might expect that David had no choice; he had been caught red handed. But remember David is still the king. He has suppressed God's notions of justice and morality before. He has even killed to cover up this indiscretion. Confession and repentance are not required here.

My friends, it takes great moral courage to face up to our sin, to admit when things about us are terribly wrong. It is not so hard to tell *other* people when they are wrong. We are more than happy to complain about the President or the Republicans or the Democrats. We are eager to announce the sins of our denomination and leaders in Louisville. We are glad to whisper about the "indiscretions" of our fellow church members. And yet, to speak the words David spoke, "*I* have sinned against the Lord," those are hard words to say. A lesser man might not have spoken at all, merely gestured the prophet into a back room, and never heard from him again; maybe even giving the prophet's head to his wife on a silver platter. Someone else in scripture does that, right?

But, David speaks. He confesses and repents. It is painful. He knows the consequences of what he has done. Finally, with great moral courage, David speaks to end the violence, the deception, and the lies. He throws himself completely on the mercy of God.

Yes, we are accountable to the Word of the Lord. God's word applies to everyone – from the shepherd to the king, from you to me. When we hear, "Thus says the Lord," it should not surprise us that we are confronted with "how far short *we* have fallen from all that God has asked us to be and to do."

But, my friends, **and this is important**, the Word of the Lord does not end in judgment. Through the "Word made flesh" God spoke once again. Not new words, but amplified words of forgiveness, life, and salvation. God spoke through a child born in Bethlehem with a vision of how life in this called community is supposed to be lived. Yes, sin has consequences; we cannot avoid that. However, "While we were sinners, Christ died for us." By the gracious and merciful self-sacrifice of the Word of God the world changes and forgiveness is possible. It is even promised to all who will confess and repent.

In a world like ours it takes great courage to confess, to repent, to end the violence, the deception, and the lies. It is a supreme sacrifice to give up our innocence, illusion of control, and power. The way of forgiveness is costly, even though the gift is free.

But a word of grace has already been spoken to you and to me. A life of joy, release, wholeness, peace, and salvation is waiting if only we are willing to respond with words that appear weak, but are so powerful. Yes, of all the words our children learn, we cannot neglect to teach them these. The world can change if you and I are willing to respond, "I have sinned against the Lord."

Deal Gently and Be Kind
2 Samuel 18:1-5

1Then David mustered the men who were with him, and set over them commanders of thousands and commanders of hundreds. 2And David divided the army into three groups: one third under the command of Joab, one third under the command of Abishai son of Zeruiah, Joab's brother, and one third under the command of Ittai the Gittite. The king said to the men, "I myself will also go out with you." 3But the men said, "You shall not go out. For if we flee, they will not care about us. If half of us die, they will not care about us. But you are worth ten thousand of us; therefore it is better that you send us help from the city." 4The king said to them, "Whatever seems best to you I will do." So the king stood at the side of the gate, while all the army marched out by hundreds and by thousands. 5The king ordered Joab and Abishai and Ittai, saying, "Deal gently for my sake with the young man Absalom." And all the people heard when the king gave orders to all the commanders concerning Absalom.

I did not watch much television as a child, but I do clearly remember every afternoon watching a man begin to sing as he walked through a door:

> *It's a beautiful day in this neighborhood,*
> *A beautiful day for a neighbor,*
> *Would you be mine?*
> *Could you be mine?*
> *Won't you be neighbor?*

And I readily said yes. Absolutely Mr. Rogers, I will be your neighbor. Thus, began a half hour of public television talking about real and significant issues with children. With both real-life dialogue and through a short trolley ride to the Land of Make Believe, Fred Rogers created a world of truth and honesty and kindness and love which acknowledged that anger, fear, and other kinds of hurt happen. He knew that children need to learn how to speak honestly about their feelings with people they trust. If that was possible in Mr. Rogers' Neighborhood, perhaps it could be in our neighborhoods too.

In this fiftieth anniversary year of the first PBS broadcast of Mr. Rogers' Neighborhood, there has been renewed interest in Fred Rogers with books and postage stamps and especially a marvelous documentary film called *Won't You Be My Neighbor*. That Fred Rogers is remembered fifty years after his first show, fifteen years after his death, is astounding. For as the show's producer Margy Whitmer says, "If you take all of the elements that make good television and do the exact opposite, you have Mr. Rogers' Neighborhood. Low production value, simple set, unlikely star, yet it worked."[68]

You may know that Fred Rogers got his start in television about the same time he enrolled in Pittsburgh Theological Seminary. He had planned on being a local church pastor, but about that time he turned on a television set for the first time. And he saw a man being hit in the face with a pie. He was aghast. How could he preach love and kindness in a church when preschoolers were absorbing such violence on TV? Once he graduated from seminary he was ordained as a Presbyterian minister to a ministry of children's television.

And what a ministry it became. If you had the privilege this summer to watch the *Won't You Be My Neighbor* documentary you will probably attest that at the end of the film there was hardly a dry eye in the theatre. Plus, usually applause. Now some of that is nostalgia. A generation that grew up watching Mr. Rogers every day on television was transported back to their childhood. But there is more to it. As film critic A.O. Scott has written,

> The most radical thing about [Fred Rogers] was his unwavering commitment to the value of kindness in the face of the world that could seem intent on devising new ways to be mean. "Let's make the most of this beautiful day," he would sing at the start of each episode. He made it sound so simple, but also as if he knew just how hard it could be.[69]

---

[68] Won't You Be My Neighbor Trailer (2018), https://youtu.be/HV_kxc9PxrQ
[69] AO Scott, "Review: Take the Next Trolley to 'Won't You Be My Neighbor?'" https://www.nytimes.com/2018/06/06/movies/wont-you-be-my-neighbor-review-mister-rogers.html

My friends, that is why I have taken some time this morning to introduce or reintroduce us to the ministry of Fred Rogers. Because we live in a world that is intent on devising new ways to be mean. And an ethic of gentleness and kindness like we see in our scripture texts for today, like we saw lived out by Fred Rogers, is truly radical.

Just think for a minute about King David and his response to the rebellion led by his own son Absalom. Their relationship had been strained for years since Absalom had killed his step-brother Amnon as revenge for Amnon's rape of Absalom's sister Tamar. Yes, this part of 2 Samuel is nothing less than a soap opera. As punishment for murder, Absalom was exiled until King David begrudgingly allowed him to return. Still, David refused to see him. The seeds of a rebellion were planted in the anger both men felt toward one another.

But that is how one is supposed to deal with opponents, at least according to our culture, right? If someone betrays you, they become your enemy. Shun them, bully them, and assassinate their character. Dismiss any word that comes out of their mouth. Devise new ways to be mean.

Theologian Christine Pohl describes this as a culture of ruthlessness. She writes:

> Ruthlessness ...comes in various forms and at multiple levels of destructiveness. ... Anyone who has dealt with middle-school bullying knows about the social power and personal consequences of focused, crushing meanness. And then there are the exhibitions of ruthlessness that are crafted for our entertainment—reality TV shows that invite the audience to enjoy contestants' pursuit of prizes that involve all manner of interpersonal betrayal. The disrespectful characterizations of opponents in contemporary public arguments and political campaigns are so common as to be almost taken for granted. ...
>
> [She continues] People of faith have their own versions of ruthlessness—usually cloaked in something good because

ruthless behavior in its raw form so obviously contradicts the gospel. We justify our unkind words or harsh actions because they are for the sake of the kingdom, the cause or the institution. Whether the disagreements are in a local church or at a global level, once we have characterized those with whom we disagree as enemies, our attempts to prevail are rarely limited by Jesus' call for love, generosity and forgiveness.[70]

Dr. Pohl wrote that in 2012, long before our current challenges at civility in the midst of a world awash in Facebook and Twitter.

Yes, if that is how the world says we are to treat our enemies, then King David should have sent his troops off with explicit instructions to take no prisoners and exact vengeance upon the rebels. But that is not what he does. With a final command heard by the entire army, David says, "Deal gently for my sake with the young man Absalom." As king he knows the rebellion must be stopped, the battle must be fought, and the throne must be reclaimed. And yet, through all that, he asks ... or does he plea ... that his generals deal gently with the young man responsible.

David obviously loved his son and wanted the best for him. His time in exile from the throne seems to have reawakened in David an understanding of the role of a king in God's kingdom. So, he asks the generals to deal gently with the young man not because he deserves it or has earned it or is worthy of such kindness. No, deal gently with the young man "for my sake," David says. You see gentleness and kindness are the character of a good king, a good shepherd, for that is the character of our God.

Presbyterian minister and author Eugene Peterson put it this way:

> Loving Absalom that day was one of the most magnificent things David ever did. The fruit of humility and prayer, it gave expression to the Son of David's best and most

---

[70] Christine Pohl, "Recovering Kindness," https://www.christiancentury.org/article/2012-10/recovering-kindness

difficult command, also given in the proximity of his betrayer: Love one another (John 13:34-35).[71]

Yes, love one another is what Jesus commanded his disciples. Yet somehow today even in the church we seem intent on devising new ways to be mean. That is why the gentleness of King David in this text, the kindness of Fred Rogers, seem both so foreign to us and so moving.

My friends, I hope you can see what a radical ethic this is. It is not just being nice. It is not tolerating difference or ignoring wrongdoing. No, it is an intentional decision to live for others. Again, Christine Pohl writes:

> In Greek ... kindness is far more than a single or random action; it is part of a way of life characterized by moral attentiveness that is both respectful of—and helpful to—others. Kindness involves a recognition of our common humanity and frailty that leads us to care about each person's particular well-being and to treat him or her as deserving of generous response and respect.[72]

That is what King David does with Absalom. Absalom deserves punishment, vengeance, ruthlessness. But King David asks his generals to show the young man some respect, to be generous, to deal gently with him. And hearing this story today, it catches us off guard. We begin to see there truly is another way to be and to live in this world.

In 1969, while the television evening news showed clips of white life guards throwing bleach into newly integrated public swimming pools where African-Americans attempted to swim, on his show Fred Rogers sat on a bench with his feet in a small plastic wading pool. One of the show's other characters, Officer Clemmons, an African-American stopped by for a visit. Mr. Rogers commented on how hot it was that day and how nice to be able to put his feet in the water. He invited Officer Clemmons to join him in his pool. And Officer

---

[71] Eugene Peterson, *Leap Over a Wall*, 204.
[72] Pohl, ibid.

Clemmons takes his off his shoes and his socks, sits down beside Mr. Rogers, and together they soak their feet in the water, side by side.[73]

My friends, gentleness and kindness are truly radical in a world set on devising new ways to be mean. Remember what Fred Rogers' producer said about his show, "Take all of the elements that make good television and do the exact opposite." Could that be God's call to Reid Memorial Presbyterian Church? Take all the elements that our culture suggests for how we treat opponents, enemies, and those with whom we disagree and do the exact opposite.

Before you tweet or like or share, ask yourself, "does this build up someone else or tear them down?"

Before you speak, ask yourself, "Will someone hear this and think, "That was so kind?"

Before you respond in ruthlessness, ask, "Is this how Jesus treats me?"

My friends, let's make the most of this beautiful day. We can be good neighbors. We can be leaders in this community with gentleness and kindness. This is our call. For as the apostle Paul wrote to the Ephesians so many years ago:

> Be kind to one another, tenderhearted, forgiving one another, as God in Christ has forgiven you. Therefore be imitators of God, as beloved children, and live in love, as Christ loved us and gave himself up for us, a fragrant offering and sacrifice to God.[74]

---

[73] NPR Staff – Morning Edition, "Walking the Beat in Mr. Rogers Neighborhood, Where a New Day Began Together," https://www.npr.org/2016/03/11/469846519/walking-the-beat-in-mr-rogers-neighborhood-where-a-new-day-began-together

[74] Ephesians 4:32-5:2

A Prayer for Wisdom
1 Kings 3:3-14

³ Solomon loved the Lord, walking in the statutes of his father David; only, he sacrificed and offered incense at the high places. ⁴ The king went to Gibeon to sacrifice there, for that was the principal high place; Solomon used to offer a thousand burnt offerings on that altar. ⁵ At Gibeon the Lord appeared to Solomon in a dream by night; and God said, "Ask what I should give you." ⁶ And Solomon said, "You have shown great and steadfast love to your servant my father David, because he walked before you in faithfulness, in righteousness, and in uprightness of heart toward you; and you have kept for him this great and steadfast love, and have given him a son to sit on his throne today. ⁷ And now, O Lord my God, you have made your servant king in place of my father David, although I am only a little child; I do not know how to go out or come in. ⁸ And your servant is in the midst of the people whom you have chosen, a great people, so numerous they cannot be numbered or counted. ⁹ Give your servant therefore an understanding mind to govern your people, able to discern between good and evil; for who can govern this your great people?"

¹⁰ It pleased the Lord that Solomon had asked this. ¹¹ God said to him, "Because you have asked this, and have not asked for yourself long life or riches, or for the life of your enemies, but have asked for yourself understanding to discern what is right, ¹² I now do according to your word. Indeed I give you a wise and discerning mind; no one like you has been before you and no one like you shall arise after you. ¹³ I give you also what you have not asked, both riches and honor all your life; no other king shall compare with you. ¹⁴ If you will walk in my ways, keeping my statutes and my commandments, as your father David walked, then I will lengthen your life."

One year for Christmas, I think I was in the third grade, what I wanted more than anything else in the entire world was … a set of encyclopedias. Yes, it is ok to laugh. Now, children and youth, you may not know what encyclopedias are – it was like Google in about 30 books. Volumes A to Z, some letters with more than one volume, but each full of articles on everything you might possibly want to know.

I had no idea how much an entire set of encyclopedias cost or whether I would actually use them after a few cursory glances at the articles that interested me. But I had a quest for knowledge and I wanted a set of encyclopedias of my own. I put them at the top of my Christmas list.

On Christmas morning as my family and I opened our presents, one at a time as everyone in our family takes turns on Christmas morning, I received some wonderful things. But when the last present had been distributed - no encyclopedias. I sat there discouraged, when my mom and dad suggested there might be one more present behind the chair. Jumping up, I discovered a large cardboard box full of books. I was ecstatic! Encyclopedias! They were not new, but there were thirty volumes, A-Z, everything I might possibly want to know. My heart's desire.

That is essentially the opportunity that Solomon has in our text for today. To receive his heart's desire. We should recognize that it is not often that God shows up and says, "Hey! It is your lucky day. Ask for anything and I will give it to you." That kind of opportunity is far more common in stories about genies popping out of lamps than with the God who created the heavens and the earth; the God who delivered the people of Israel from slavery in Egypt; and the God who died on the cross to set us free from sin and death. In fact, I usually rant against such vending machine theology – you know, put your money in, punch a button, and God will give you exactly what you want. God as a vending machine. But never say never. At Gibeon the Lord appeared to Solomon in a dream at night and gives him the chance to ask for anything he wants.

Given this chance, for what would you ask? What is your heart's desire? The assumption in the text seems to be that Solomon is going to ask for riches or long life or deliverance from his enemies. And that is a good assumption to make. That is the kind of king the prophet Samuel warned the people of Israel about when they first asked for a king.[75] Their first two kings, Saul and David, certainly

---

[75] 1 Samuel 8

had moments of self-indulgence exactly along these lines. So, what is to prevent Solomon from being any different?

Our culture seems to believe that, if given the chance, we would ask for similar things as well. And it is not a bad assumption. What is our heart's desire – a second home in the mountains or at the beach? Enough money to quit your job or at least ensure you can travel in your retirement? Maybe to get rid of that person who most annoys you at work or who keeps posting such absurd political beliefs on Facebook? Yes, there are many people in the world who would request exactly that kind of physical and material excess.

And yet I suspect, and not just because you are sitting in worship pondering, that with at least a second thought you might have something different in mind. If you could ask God for anything and know that your wish would be granted, perhaps you would request the healing of a broken relationship? Or maybe the cure for a devastating disease that has afflicted you or someone you love? Maybe one more day with someone that you have lost. Or perhaps you would ask for the easing of some burden? Or maybe your request would be for someone else like your children or grandchildren. But I suspect that most of us would request something more than riches, long life, or deliverance from enemies.

And with a little more pondering, we may even ask for something else. Solomon asks for "an understanding mind to govern [God's] people, able to discern between good and evil." I wonder if that is pretty close to what we would eventually ask for as well. Maybe not in the moment, mind you, but with a minute or two of reflection. Because I must tell you, people who come to see me as their pastor rarely ask for how they can get more money, or live longer, or smite their enemies. They probably know I cannot help them with that.

But they do come asking for any guidance I might have about how they can do the right thing in the midst of whatever dilemma or challenge they face. They want to make the right choice. They want to do the godly thing. They are not looking for the kind of wisdom and knowledge that one finds in encyclopedias. No, they are looking for the wisdom to do what God wants them to do.

That is what Solomon is asking for when he prays for an "understanding mind." In fact, "understanding mind" is a horrible translation of the original Hebrew. It makes sense for us in the 21st century because we think that decision making happens in our heads. We have great trust in our minds and our reason to figure out what is best in every situation. But the writers of the Old Testament knew better. They knew that no matter how rational we believe ourselves to be, the heart will trump our mind every time.

Solomon wants to be a good king; he wants to rule God's people well. So, Solomon literally asks for a "hearing heart." Yes, a hearing heart - a heart that listens to God. He seeks a reason that understands; an instinct for the truth. He wants to be able to do what is right and avoid what is wrong. And to do that he needs not just head knowledge; he needs a heart in tune with God's will.

A heart in tune with God's will – that is what Scripture means by "wisdom." It is not just the kind of head knowledge that comes from memorizing the Ten Commandments or the Apostles' Creed. If that was the case then no one would ever come and ask me what is the right thing to do in the midst of a dilemma. Or if they did, it would certainly make my job a lot easier - I could tell them to go memorize something.

But if we are to live a faithful life, we need far more than a simple yes or no, right or left, check the correct box kind of ethics. As Presbyterian pastor, and my friend, Rev. Jack Haberer has written,

> What is needed for believers is not a singular strategy to discover the one right thing God has planned but the cultivation of the kind of wisdom with which one can make godly decisions about what one should do. What one needs is to so imbibe the mind of Christ as revealed in Scripture that one can be conversant with and attentive to the guidance provided by the revealed words of God. Of course, actually learning God's will through the reading of

the Bible is more easily said than done. That book is complicated, just as life is complicated.[76]

Yes, the quest for wisdom presses us to be good students of God's Word, not because it contains all the instructions we need for living, but because it is the primary way that God continues to speak afresh to our hearts. We cannot just read it or memorize it once and say we are done. We need to go back to the Scriptures again and again and again and again. For we will never be masters of what God has revealed and is revealing to us in the Word.

So, our prayer is for wisdom is for a "hearing heart," continually open to the mind of Christ being poured out for us through the Word.

Our prayer for wisdom is for eyes to see and ears to hear what God seeks to teach us this day.

Our prayer for wisdom is for the imagination to hear the old, old story in new and surprising ways.

Our prayer for wisdom is that our hearts might be so in tune with God's heart that we are not always asking, "what should I do?" because deep in our hearts we know what is right, and what is good, and what is just.

In short, our prayer for wisdom is that we might be willing to walk with God not just once, but every minute of every day.

My friends, there is far more to know than can be contained in all the encyclopedias and all the Google searches. May we pray for a "hearing heart," that we might truly be wise.

---

[76] Jack Haberer, *It's Complicated: A Guide to Faithful Decision Making*, 8-9.

Part 4

Trying to Say What is True

Astounded and Amazed
Mark 1:21-28

21 They went to Capernaum; and when the sabbath came, he entered the synagogue and taught. 22 They were astounded at his teaching, for he taught them as one having authority, and not as the scribes. 23 Just then there was in their synagogue a man with an unclean spirit, 24 and he cried out, "What have you to do with us, Jesus of Nazareth? Have you come to destroy us? I know who you are, the Holy One of God." 25 But Jesus rebuked him, saying, "Be silent, and come out of him!" 26 And the unclean spirit, convulsing him and crying with a loud voice, came out of him. 27 They were all amazed, and they kept on asking one another, "What is this? A new teaching—with authority! He commands even the unclean spirits, and they obey him." 28 At once his fame began to spread throughout the surrounding region of Galilee.

They were all astounded at his teaching. They were all amazed after the unclean spirit came out of the man, convulsing him and crying out with a loud voice as he went. "What is this?" they asked. Yes, Jesus shows up in the synagogue and people are astounded and amazed. And at once his fame began to spread throughout the surrounding region of Galilee.

Pretty impressive for the first century Galilee, but I am not sure Jesus would have even been a blip on anyone's radar today.

For we live in a culture awash in fame and celebrity. Much of it is centered online. For example, how many Twitter followers do you need to become famous? I thought I was doing pretty well with just over 500 followers on Twitter. But then I learned that pop singer Katie Perry has 108,474,494 followers on Twitter.[77] She is famous. For those not versed in Twitter, that means all those followers can read quotes by and get news about Katie Perry – everything from a video of her singing to a picture of what she had for breakfast to her thoughts on whatever topic might catch her interest today. More than 108 million people. That is amazing. And just so you know,

---

[77] https://twittercounter.com/pages/100 on January 28, 2018, 8:33 AM

Jesus does appear to have a few Twitter accounts, but I suspect he gets someone else to send tweets for him.

Now, there are some other ways to become famous online. On Tuesday *The Telegraph*, a London newspaper, shared a recent survey of career aspirations for United Kingdom elementary-aged children. The top three choices were not too surprising: sports star, teacher, and veterinarian. But the next one might astound you. "Social media and video game star" was the fourth most popular choice.[78] Yes, these elementary aged children want to be YouTube celebrities or professional video game players. And the scary thing is, while I have no idea how it is possible, you can actually make a living doing that today. "Social media and video game star?" Perhaps those are the career aspirations of some of our children in the Mothers' Day Out and Preschool program? Maybe young Milly (whom we baptized today) will grow up to do that? If so, parents don't say I didn't warn you! Yes, social media and video game star far outpaced being a doctor, a lawyer, or owning a business. And as far as I can tell "carpenter in Galilee" did not make the list. Astounding.

Yes, I am not sure Jesus could compete in such a world of Twitter, YouTube, and video games. We seem much more enamored with people who are famous not for any particular skill or accomplishment or worthwhile word, but who are famous just for being famous. Even in the church we have turned preachers into celebrities with bestselling books and conferences and videos. Even the Pope has a Twitter account and I am posting YouTube videos each week to encourage you, and through you your friends, to come to worship on Sunday.

In his book, *American Idols: The Worship of the American Dream*, Bob Hostetler, suggests three things are at the root of Americans' fascination with celebrityism: the longings for community, significance, and glory. He writes:

---

[78] Mike Wright, "How easy is it to become a YouTube Star? The career of choice for today's school children,"
http://www.telegraph.co.uk/technology/2018/01/23/easy-become-youtube-star-career-choice-todays-school-children/

We feel connected to celebrities even though they don't know us. It's almost that they become our friends ... even though we have no idea who these people are and what they're really like. It underscores the lack of community many of us feel. Obviously, all three [longings] are God's will for us, but it's not His will to find it in celebrity worship.[79]

If it is not God's will for us to find community, significance, and glory in celebrity worship; if we might even more accurately call that idolatry; can we find them in a first century Jewish carpenter in a synagogue in Capernaum? Does that Jesus still astound and amaze even today?

Remember that Jesus arrived in Capernaum with his four disciples. As soon as he announces that the Kingdom of God has drawn near, he begins to invite others to be a part of it. They leave their nets and follow him. They begin to form a community. And notice Jesus does not take these disciples, this new community, someplace apart and separate. No, he takes them to Capernaum, to their hometown, to their daily lives, to the synagogue where they worshiped. And there he begins to teach, inviting still others to join this new community.

Well, that community grows and grows, sometimes for the better and sometimes for the worse, but it grows. It is passed down, generation to generation until we find that we have gathered here in this sanctuary this morning. If we are longing for community and relationships of meaning, then we should be astounded by the fact that the same community that gathered in that synagogue so many years ago still gathers today. In a world where so much focus and attention is placed on the individual, it is amazing that we might see Jesus by turning our attention to those who still gather to seek him. Yes, to see Jesus, to find relationships of meaning, we need to become connected with and engaged in the life of the church, the community of faith.

---

[79] Quoted by Brett McCracken, https://relevantmagazine.com/culture/tv/features/22238-the-cult-of-celebrity

And then while teaching in that synagogue the really interesting part of this story happens. Jesus is approached by a man who suffered from an unclean spirit. I don't know about you, but talking about unclean spirits seems so foreign to us because we live in a world where we expect everything can be fixed with the right prescription, procedure, or therapy. That is how it works for the celebrities, right? But however we understand unclean spirits, what is most important to this particular episode in Capernaum is that the unclean spirit sees Jesus as a threat. And he is. Because the Kingdom of God breaks into our world in ways that overturn oppression, thwart injustice, and restore wholeness to those who are suffering. Thus, Jesus ministry of healing is not an afterthought – it is an integral demonstration that the kingdom of God is here.

My friends, if we are longing for significance, we need to look not to Twitter or YouTube, but for where the kingdom of God is drawing near; where the boundary between heaven and earth is showing cracks; where we find people fighting for justice and healing; people repenting for prejudice and speaking the truth. For that is where Jesus is still at work today.

This weekend I read an op-ed in the *New York Times* by Rachael Denhollander, the first woman to publicly accuse Michigan State University and US Gymnastics doctor, Larry Nassar, of abuse. She had been abused as a fifteen-year-old teenager seeking treatment from Nassar for a chronic back injury. Now, an attorney and mother of three; finally convinced that someone might believe her, she came forward in August 2016. Since that time more than 200 women have alleged abuse by Nassar. He was sentenced this week to 175 years in prison. What courage and faith it took for Denhollander to file her police report, to speak the truth, to seek justice. But she paid a price. She writes,

> My education as a lawyer prepared me for the process and presentation. But absolutely nothing could have prepared me for the pain of being the first to go public with my accusations … I lost my church. I lost my closest friends as a result of advocating for survivors who had been victimized

by similar institutional failures in my own community. I lost every shred of privacy.[80]

And yet, at the sentencing hearing for Nassar, Denhollander was the final victim to speak. While asking the judge for the fullest sentence, she included this word to Nassar himself:

> Should you ever reach the point of truly facing what you have done, the guilt will be crushing. And that is what makes the gospel of Christ so sweet. Because it extends grace and hope and mercy where none should be found. And it will be there for you.
>
> I pray you experience the soul crushing weight of guilt so you may someday experience true repentance and true forgiveness from God, which you need far more than forgiveness from me — though I extend that to you as well.[81]

That is a life of healing. That is a life of significance. That is a life of truth. That is a life where Jesus may be found. Astounding and amazing us even today.

For my friends, the glory we truly long for is not for a quick fifteen minutes of fame on the internet. No matter how many likes and hearts and views we get, no matter how many people know our name, true glory comes when we help to set a brother or sister free. That is what Jesus did in the synagogue. That is what astounded and amazed the crowd back then. And that is what Jesus is still doing

---

[80] Rachael Denhollander, "Rachael Denhollander: The Price I Paid for Taking On Larry Nassar,"
https://www.nytimes.com/2018/01/26/opinion/sunday/larry-nassar-rachael-denhollander.html
[81] Rachael Denhollander, "Read Rachael Denhollander's full victim impact statement about Larry Nassar,"
https://www.cnn.com/2018/01/24/us/rachael-denhollander-full-statement/index.html

today. Astounding and amazing. And inviting us to join him in all that is to come.

The Faith that Lives in You
2 Timothy 1:1-10

Ordination and Installation of W. Dayton Wilson

Before we read our second scripture this afternoon, I must begin with a word of thanks for I am honored and humbled to be here. Yes, thank you to the Session and Congregation of First Presbyterian Church, to the commission of North Alabama Presbytery, and certainly to my friend and brother in faith Dayton Wilson for the invitation to be with you this afternoon on this most joyous occasion.

Dayton and Michelle and Sarah and I have a long history. When I first moved to Lumberton, NC in January 2007, I learned there was a wedding on the church calendar for March 17th. Well, I had something on my personal calendar for March 19th – that was the due date for the birth of our youngest child. But, by God's grace, and a little scheduling with the OBGYN, our daughter Bekah was born on March 7th and I had the honor of marrying Dayton and Michelle on the 17th.

It was then my honor to baptize little D, who is not so little any more, on the same day as we baptized his cousin Jace. Dayton moderated the Deacons, he served as an elder. I presided at the funerals for Dayton's grandmother and his mother. One of my last acts as pastor in Lumberton was to marry Coble D and Jill. Yes, the roots and connections with the Wilson family are deep.

Of all the time we spent together, I still remember quite clearly the day when Dayton sent me an email which said, "I have some questions and I think you are the one who has the answers." We made an appointment in the next day or so and Dayton came in, sat down in my office, and we started talking about ministry. And by God's amazing grace, a lot of prayer and hard work, and the wondrous gifts of Dayton and this congregation of call, here we are today.

I have thought a lot about this day and the best way I can describe being with you this afternoon is to say that most of you know that I now pastor in Augusta, Georgia. And this weekend there is a little golf tournament being played there. Last year on the second Sunday of April, my son Sam and I spent the afternoon following Jordan Spieth and Ricky Fowler around the back nine, before watching Sergio Garcia win in a playoff on the 18th green. It was an unforgettable day. And while there is a pretty good chance that I could be at the National again today, I would so much rather be right here with all of you as we ordain and install Dayton Wilson as a Minister of Word and Sacrament.

But enough words of introduction, let us turn our hearts and minds to hear the Word of the Lord found this afternoon in Paul's second letter to Timothy, the first chapter, verses 1-10.

> *1 Paul, an apostle of Christ Jesus by the will of God, for the sake of the promise of life that is in Christ Jesus,*

> *2 To Timothy, my beloved child:*

> *Grace, mercy, and peace from God the Father and Christ Jesus our Lord.*

> *3 I am grateful to God—whom I worship with a clear conscience, as my ancestors did—when I remember you constantly in my prayers night and day. 4 Recalling your tears, I long to see you so that I may be filled with joy. 5 I am reminded of your sincere faith, a faith that lived first in your grandmother Lois and your mother Eunice and now, I am sure, lives in you. 6 For this reason I remind you to rekindle the gift of God that is within you through the laying on of my hands;7 for God did not give us a spirit of cowardice, but rather a spirit of power and of love and of self-discipline.*

> *8 Do not be ashamed, then, of the testimony about our Lord or of me his prisoner, but join with me in suffering for the gospel, relying on the power of God, 9 who saved us and called us with a holy calling, not according to our works but according to his own purpose and grace. This grace was given to us in Christ Jesus before the ages began, 10 but it has now been revealed through the appearing of our Savior Christ*

Jesus, who abolished death and brought life and immortality to light through the gospel.

Do you remember who it was who first told you about Jesus? Who it was who taught you to sing Jesus Loves Me? Who it was that gave you your first Bible? Whether you were young or grown, who it was that told you the stories of creation, and the flood, and King David, and angels and shepherds and wise men and a manger, a cross and an empty tomb? Yes, do you remember?

For some of you that person or persons might be very clear. Yes, perhaps you did not grow up in the faith, so at some point someone told you about Jesus. You made a clear decision for Jesus and your life changed dramatically as a result.

But there are others, and I suspect we have a good number of you with us this afternoon, who have always been a part of a church family. You cannot remember a time when you were not a part of the church, maybe even this church. So, if you cannot remember the first person to tell you stories about Jesus, that's ok. You have always been a part of the church and there are numerous folks who have shared the story of faith with you.

Comedian and late-night talk show host Stephen Colbert talks about how his family shared the faith with him:

> I go to church and am somewhat religious and when I try to explain to some people who aren't that I have a belief, I say, "Well, I was given this by my ancestors." I look at my children and I go, I love them, I wouldn't want to give them anything that I didn't think would help them. So I assume I was given this by my ancestors because they gave it to me to try to help me. And I open it like a box, and I wonder what's inside, but I don't think I've gotten to the bottom at any point.[82]

---

[82] Laura Darling, "Stephen Colbert on the Transmission of Faith," http://www.confirmnotconform.com/blog/stephen-colbert-transmission-faith

Yes, someone in your life has given you this wonderful gift, especially if you have been born and nurtured in the church. And at some point, we all have to decide if faith is going to become real for us; if we are going to open the box and unwrap the great gift of our ancestors; if we are going to say yes to God in the same way that God has said yes to us.

In our scripture text this afternoon the apostle Paul writes to Timothy in order to remind him that this gift of faith was first seen in Timothy's grandmother Lois and then in his mother Eunice, and now it lives in Timothy himself. Timothy opened that gift and it now lives in him. Yes, the gift of faith, of trust, of good news, of sound teaching, of sure words; this good treasure has been entrusted to Timothy so that he might guard it and keep it. The word here in Greek is *phylaxon* and it is the same word used to describe the task of the shepherds in Luke's Gospel as they "*keep watch* over the flock by night." Yes, Timothy was to "keep watch" over this treasure of the gospel, to shepherd it and nurture it. Such is the task of each generation, to keep the faith entrusted to us so that it grows and flourishes until we might pass it on to others.

And even more than that, as we keep the faith that lives in us, we become an active part of a people trying together to do the same thing; a people continually saved and delivered by God, a people with tradition. For from the Latin *traditio*, tradition means "assumptions, beliefs, patterns of behavior handed down from the past." To value our "tradition" is to remember that all we have is a gift to us; it has been handed down to us from those who have walked this way before. To remember our "tradition" is to recognize that we are not the first ones to have ever read the scriptures; we are not the first ones to ever gather for worship; and we are not the first ones to ever struggle with living a Christian life in the midst of a complicated world. Yes, we have much to learn and there is much to be treasured in all that has been handed down to us.

Paul reminds Timothy that his faith was handed on to him from his grandmother and his mother. While those of you here in Athens, Alabama did not have the privilege, I was blessed to be able to know the faith that was handed onto to Dayton by his grandmother

Virginia and his mother Pattie. I can tell you that they were women of deep and passionate faith. Virginia was in her final years when I knew her, but she could still make things happen in Lumberton, NC. If I wanted to know anything about anyone in the church all I had to do was stop by to visit Virginia. And if the time between my visits had become, in her opinion, too long she would call up to the church office and ask me to come. Virginia knew all these things about everyone not because she was a gossip; no, because she loved them all so well. At her funeral she wouldn't let me talk about her. No she wanted a sermon about how we love because God first loved us. That faith and love Virginia passed on to Dayton.

When I think about the faith of Pattie, I think about how Pattie could pray. Oh, how she could pray. She prayed for her boys – for Coble and for Dayton. Pattie recognized this call to ministry in Dayton long before he or I ever did and she prayed and she prayed and she prayed that what we are celebrating today would become a reality. In the notes she left for her funeral Pattie clearly said, "Read Psalm 23. Have a sermon not about me but to invite someone to God. Love you all!" That's the kind of firm and certain faith which resulted in a life of prayer and worship that Pattie passed on to Dayton.

Yes, Dayton the faith of your grandmother and the faith of your mother, plus the faith of your father and Jill, your aunts and uncles, your pastors, your professors, your friends, and perhaps most importantly now Michelle lives in you. And you as members of First Presbyterian Church - the same is true for you! The faith of your grandparents, your mothers and fathers, your children, your pastors, now lives in you.

However, if we are not careful, if we fail to keep it, we too easily forget this is a living faith. When that happens, faith can become firm and rote. A friend of mine who is often invited to speak and preach at churches around the country tells the story of preaching in a particular congregation one Sunday.[83] The worship service was quite inspiring and the congregation was quite attentive during his sermon. After he finished preaching my friend sat down and the

---

[83] Dr. Rodger Nishioka told this story when I interned with him more than 20 years ago.

church's minister invited the congregation to stand and repeat the Apostles' Creed. Everyone stood up, turned to look at the back of the sanctuary, and began to recite the creed.

Initially puzzled, but after thinking about it for the remainder of the service, my friend became quite impressed with this practice. He thought the theological foundation for turning around to speak the creed must be that the congregation had heard the Word of God and now was declaring to the world what it believed and pledging to carry that Word with them into the week ahead. He wanted to share this practice with other churches around the country, so he asked the pastor after the service if he was right about the thinking behind everyone turning around for the creed. The pastor smiled and said, no. That was not it at all. For years and years a large hand-made banner hung on the back wall of the sanctuary with the words of the Apostles' Creed. Everyone turned around so they could read the words. Yet, five years ago, the sanctuary had been remodeled. The banner had been taken down and never re-hung. Still every Sunday the congregation stands and turns around to recite the creed just as it had for generations.

As amusing as that story is, it is also frightening, isn't it? It is scary that our living faith, our traditional expressions and statements of faith can become rote, mechanical, and lifeless. For many, especially in the church, a living faith has because something fixed and distant, a kind of endowment that must not be touched. Tradition and faith are something to be admired, but not handled. Tradition and faith are something to inform new members about, but not really something to "hand on" to them. Thus, tradition and faith become a mental exercise of remembering events which happened long ago, not an actual experience of salvation and deliverance. Tradition and faith fail to be a way to know the past so that eyes might be opened to see God at work in the present. For so many, in the name of holding on to our tradition and faith, we have forgotten how to pass them on.

That is one of the reasons we need pastors, or perhaps a better way to put it would be to say that is one of the reasons God calls pastors for the church. For one of the calls of a pastor is to help us see the intersections of our stories with God's story, to inspire us to pass on the tradition and faith of the church not in a rote, mechanical, and lifeless way, but in a way that is fluid, impassioned, and life-giving. Yes, we need pastors to nurture and kindle the faith that lives in you.

Dayton, the faith of your grandmother and your mother now lives in you. First Presbyterian Church, the faith of your ancestors now lives in you. Together you can keep this faith alive and share it with the generations which are to come.

This is a sacred calling. And yet, at its heart it remains the same as the song someone taught us to sing as children:

> *Jesus loves me! This I know, For the Bible tells me so;*
> *Little ones to Him belong; They are weak, but He is strong.*
> *Yes, Jesus loves me! Yes, Jesus loves me!*
> *Yes, Jesus loves me! The Bible tells me so.*

When the Advocate Comes
John 15:26-27 and 16:4b-11

Pentecost – Graduates Sunday

26 "When the Advocate comes, whom I will send to you from the Father, the Spirit of truth who comes from the Father, he will testify on my behalf. 27 You also are to testify because you have been with me from the beginning. ...

4b "I did not say these things to you from the beginning, because I was with you. 5 But now I am going to him who sent me; yet none of you asks me, 'Where are you going?' 6 But because I have said these things to you, sorrow has filled your hearts. 7 Nevertheless I tell you the truth: it is to your advantage that I go away, for if I do not go away, the Advocate will not come to you; but if I go, I will send him to you. 8 And when he comes, he will prove the world wrong about sin and righteousness and judgment: 9 about sin, because they do not believe in me; 10 about righteousness, because I am going to the Father and you will see me no longer; 11 about judgment, because the ruler of this world has been condemned.

It is quite appropriate that this morning is Pentecost and also the day we celebrate our high school and college graduates. Because Pentecost is a day of new beginnings; a day in which, through the gift of the Holy Spirit, the plans and promises of God begin to unfold in new and surprising ways. Yes, Pentecost is a day of possibility and promise.

And that is what we celebrate with our graduates, right? The future is unlimited; the possibilities are endless. It is as if you have reached the edge of the map and the best years of your life are just a step or two away into the unknown which is yet to be charted. Yes, it is time to celebrate.

All of that is true and yet I do not want you to be unaware that at least somewhere or someday in that uncharted future you will hit a moment of pause. Despite the courage and bravado of graduation, someday you will encounter a minute of uncertainty and even a bit of fear. That moment comes for us all, time and time again, no matter how long ago our graduations might have been.

One such moment, of many in my own life, came the night before my first day of class as a freshman at Davidson College. As I assume is still the case, during orientation Davidson freshmen are given the opportunity to demonstrate their proficiency, or lack thereof, in a foreign language. I had taken French in high school, so I sat for the French exam. My score came back much better than I anticipated. In high school we spent our time learning to read French, but rarely ever spoke it. However, due to my score, my advisor placed me in a third level French conversation class. Needless to say, I was quite concerned about this development and went to bed very troubled the night before the first day of class.

Now I am not sure that I have shared this bit of personal information with you before, but after five years as your pastor you are probably entitled to know that in times of great stress, change, or transition in my life, I tend to sleepwalk. As the story goes, on that night before class at about three o'clock in the morning I jumped out of bed, opened the door to my dorm room, and walked down the hall to my resident advisor's room. I knocked on his door for several minutes before he opened it, rubbing the sleep from his eyes. When he asked me what was the matter I began to tell him that I had discovered the secret for how all Davidson freshmen could pass French. He looked puzzled as to why I was sharing this information with him at three o'clock in the morning, but he asked anyway, "So Matt, what is the secret?"

At this point I woke up, totally confused as to where I was and what in the world I was doing. So, without a word I turned around and went back to bed. Unfortunately, I never again discovered the "secret" to passing French - at least anything more secret than a lot of hard work and hours of time spent in the language lab.

Our scripture text for this morning is something like that moment before the first day of class for the disciples. Throughout his teaching at the final supper, Jesus repeatedly tells the disciples that he is going away. It is going to be a new day, a graduation of sorts for them. Yet, as preacher Fred Craddock has written,

> His followers are confused. They are children playing on the floor only to look up and see Mom and Dad putting on their coats. The children have three questions, always three questions: Where are you going? Can we come? Then who will stay with us? Jesus responds, "I am going to my Father and your Father. You cannot come now; you can come later. But I will not leave you orphans. I will send another friend, another helper who will never leave, but who will stay with you forever."[84]

My friends, graduates, that is the secret, that is the promise of Pentecost – that even as we graduate and take new steps into a future that has not yet been charted, we are not left alone. For another helper who will never leave; a helper who will stay with us forever is on the way.

The Gospel of John calls this helper the *Paraclete*, the Advocate, the one who appears on another's behalf. Yes, the Holy Spirit, the Advocate, will remind us of all that Jesus has said and will lead us to the truth. As Pastor Isaac Villegas writes:

> Jesus tells his friends. "When the Spirit of truth comes, he will guide you into all the truth." And the truth is that he loves them—that he will always long for them, that he cannot imagine his life without theirs, that his soul groans with sighs too deep for words at the thought of them. Jesus reassures his beloved friends that in his absence the Paraclete will deliver his love notes to them, words written on their hearts.[85]

---

[84] Fred Craddock, "More than Anything in the World," *The Collected Sermons of Fred B. Craddock*, 187.

[85] Isaac Villegas, "May 20, Pentecost B (John 15:26-27; 16:4b-15)" https://www.christiancentury.org/article/living-word/may-20-pentecost-b-john-1526-27-164b-15

And Lord knows we need that reminder of his love. For when the Advocate comes we take those first steps beyond the map and into the world to share the love of Christ with so many who are hurting. It is not easy work. There will be times of uncertainty and fear because the divisions, despair, and distrust in the world today threaten to overwhelm us, to make us forget all that Jesus has said and done, and to think that we cannot make a difference. But it is simply not true. The Advocate, the Holy Spirit will lead us into all the truth. And the truth is that we are loved, we are not alone, and we can show the world a better way.

At the end of Brian McLaren's novel, *A New Kind of Christian*, after a long struggle and with the help of a new friend, a pastor named Dan finds his faith and hope restored. He is ready to set out on a new ministry. Talking with his wife about his decision and requesting her blessing during a winter's evening walk he says,

> "I don't know where this path will lead. It's like we've come to the edge of the map, and all familiar paths are behind us, but a new world is out there ahead of us. I feel this urge to try to find other people who are at the edge of the map too, and maybe if we travel on together we can make some new discoveries, and help each other, and ---"

> His wife stopped walking and looked up toward the next street light. "It's kind of like the snow tonight, isn't it, Dan? There aren't any footprints to follow, but there's light ahead, and there's a certain beauty in it all."[86]

My friends, on this Graduates Sunday, at the edge of the map, at the end of the old world and the beginning of a new, we find the Advocate, the Holy Spirit, who comes and stands beside us. As together we take new steps to bring love to this crazy world, there are not footprints to follow, but there is light ahead – the light of the world – and there is a certain beauty in it all. So, do not be afraid.

---

[86] Brian McLaren, *A New Kind of Christian: A Tale of Two Friends on a Spiritual Journey*, 142.

Keep your eyes wide open. Join hands. Trust that the Spirit will lead us into all the truth and the love of Jesus Christ our Lord.

What Can Separate Us?
Psalm 137:1-6 and Romans 8:31-39

Sunday after the death of 17-year-old Sarah Rhoads

Psalm 137:1-6

"By the rivers of Babylon—
there we sat down and there we wept
when we remembered Zion.
2 On the willows there
we hung up our harps.
3 For there our captors
asked us for songs,
and our tormentors asked for mirth, saying,
"Sing us one of the songs of Zion!"

4 How could we sing the LORD's song
in a foreign land?
5 If I forget you, O Jerusalem,
let my right hand wither!
6 Let my tongue cling to the roof of my mouth,
if I do not remember you,
if I do not set Jerusalem
above my highest joy.

Romans 8:31-39

31 What then are we to say about these things? If God is for us, who is against us? 32 He who did not withhold his own Son, but gave him up for all of us, will he not with him also give us everything else? 33 Who will bring any charge against God's elect? It is God who justifies. 34 Who is to condemn? It is Christ Jesus, who died, yes, who was raised, who is at the right hand of God, who indeed intercedes for us. 35 Who will separate us from the love of Christ? Will hardship, or distress, or persecution, or famine, or nakedness, or peril, or sword? 36 As it is written, "For your sake we are being killed all day long; we are accounted as sheep to be slaughtered."

143

37 No, in all these things we are more than conquerors through him who loved us. 38 For I am convinced that neither death, nor life, nor angels, nor rulers, nor things present, nor things to come, nor powers, 39 nor height, nor depth, nor anything else in all creation, will be able to separate us from the love of God in Christ Jesus our Lord.

"How could we sing the Lord's song in a foreign land?" God's people found themselves sitting not within the walls of the temple in Jerusalem, but beside the rivers of Babylon. They had been dislocated. Carried far from home and not by choice. Everything they thought they knew - gone. They could envision a future no different from that day. They did not want this. They did not plan for this. They did not expect this. Pain, hurt, tears, loss. Scripture calls it ... exile.

Yes, exile. It is not an experience unique to God's people in Babylon all those many years ago. As one commentator puts it, exile is "a cultural and spiritual condition where one feels at odds with the dominant values of the prevailing cultural ethos."[87] So to be in exile is to feel disconnected from what we have always known, to wonder about terrifying new realities of loss or conflict, to question whether this feeling of "dis-ease" will ever pass. Yes, anyone can be in exile, everyone can be in exile, even if we lay our heads down in our own beds each and every night.

My friends, I know that throughout this week I have been asking myself, "How can we sing the Lord's song in this exile?" For this is not the week that any of us had planned. This is not the Sunday that we had anticipated. Associate Pastor Nadine Ellsworth-Moran was supposed to be preaching this morning as we continued through our summer lectionary series on Samuel, Saul, David, and Solomon. That all went out the window on Wednesday morning when Sarah Rhoads' car ran head on into a log truck on the Little River Bridge. We suddenly found ourselves in exile. We did not want it. We did not plan for it. We did not expect it. Pain, hurt, tears, loss. ... Exile.

---

[87] Lee Beach, "The Church in Exile: Being a Missionary to the Dominant Culture," *Congregations* (Vol. 34, no. 4: Fall 2008) 7.

And this morning we have gathered seeking to hear a word from the Lord. If we are honest we come with this longing every Sunday for exile always threatens God's people. Tragedy hit close to home for us this week, but we are not alone in experiencing suffering. Indeed, the statistics on tragedy and suffering can easily overwhelm us. Millions of children in the United States live in poverty; almost 30,000 children around the world die of preventable diseases every day;[88] more than 750 million people in the world live on less than two dollars a day.[89] If we stop for a moment and consider all the tragedy in the world, and the number of people who suffer every day … Exile.

While the worldwide scope of tragedy and suffering can be overwhelming, it is my experience that the majority of those who seek pastoral counsel do so because they experience the sort of suffering that we have known this week, yes tragedy much closer to home. For all it takes is one suspicious text on your boyfriend's phone. One bag of marijuana found hidden beneath your child's mattress. One friend laid off from work. One argument at church that ends in tears. One person in your family diagnosed with cancer. One night wide awake in bed because the one you have loved longer than you can remember will never lay his head on the other pillow again. One telephone call from the state police at an accident scene. All it takes is one.

So whether it is thousands, millions, billions, or just one … Exile.

And when we are in exile, we get anxious. And when we get anxious, despair threatens to take over. And when despair overwhelms, we begin to fear that the future is fixed or that it will be even worse than today. And when the future is fixed, when we are gripped by fear, we start trying to just survive. We really do not know what to do. We work harder at the things that we have always done. But so often, despite our best efforts, nothing changes; things do get worse, we worry more, and survival becomes paramount. Pain, hurt, tears, loss. … Exile.

---

[88] https://www.unicef.org/mdg/childmortality.html
[89] https://www.worldbank.org/en/topic/poverty/overview

But, my friends, there is another response that the church can make in exile. Another response when we feel anxiety rising within us. Another response when the tragedy threatens to overwhelm us. It is a response of memory and hope. It is a prophetic response which sees God still at work. For as theologian Ephraim Radner writes of the people of Israel's exile to Babylon, "Exile is also a moment by which our God delineated deliverance. As such it can hardly be a cause for fear."[90]

Yes, in our own individual lives, if we are paying attention, we often see God most clearly in those darkest moments. The same is true for the people of God. In the exile of Egypt, God hears the cries of his people and delivers them. In the exile of Babylon, God hears the cries of his people and does a new thing to bring them home. In the exile of Roman occupation of Palestine, God hears the cries of his people and comes himself in Jesus Christ to deliver and save. And my friends, God hears our cries too. ... Hope!

For despite the challenge, confusion, and disorientation that exile always brings, as pastor and theologian Lee Beach writes, we will find our way through "not because we are so astute, but because God is always faithful to his promises and is constantly working in new and innovative ways."[91]

That is worth hearing again – we will find our way through exile not because **we** are so astute, but because ***God is always faithful***. We do not have the resources to survive the exile on our own, but God is always faithful. ... Hope!

In the midst of the exile of his own day, this is what the apostle Paul reminds the young fledgling church in Rome. He begins with a question of his own: "What then are we to say about these things? If God is for us, who is against us?" For Paul that is a rhetorical question. He knows the answer - God is for us; no one can stand against us - because God has demonstrated God's grace in the gift of Jesus Christ. God did not withhold his own Son, but gave him up for all of us. God gave his only Son for us so that things might be

---

[90] Quoted by Lee Beach, Ibid, 10.
[91] Ibid.

put right again, not because God had to, but because God wanted to give us a great gift. ... Hope!

Now, the giving of God's own Son was certainly not easy. Our God knows what it is like to lose a child. As we have experienced this week, there is no greater loss than that. Flesh of your own flesh, bone of your own bone. And more than just dropping him off at the airport for a trip, the giving of God's own Son was a giving to death on the cross. A humiliating death for a common criminal. But for God death was not the final word. Exile is never the final word. Resurrection follows death and opens the door to eternal life and a renewed relationship with God here and now. So, Paul asks, "Who is to condemn us for our sin? It is Christ Jesus, who died, yes, who was raised, who is at the right hand of God, who intercedes for us." This is the song of faith that we sing. God gave us the gift of his own Son so that Christ Jesus might die for us, be raised for us, sit with God forever for us, and pray for us.

This is the song of God's faithfulness. And if we believe it, then even in the midst of our deepest exile, in our deepest pain, hurt, tears, and loss, we can live and witness with confidence ... Hope!

Paul's witness in the midst of exile goes like this: "Who will separate us from the love of Christ? Will hardship, or distress, or persecution, or famine, or nakedness, or peril, or sword?" All things that we as human beings do to one another or to ourselves. Can any of these things separate us from the love of Christ? Paul says, "No! In all these things we are more than conquerors through him who loved us." All these things which we may think of as signs of God's displeasure with us: Hard times financially, distress in our families or emotions, persecution, hunger, being without the right clothes, danger, or even war. We are conquerors of all these things through God who loves us. God is for us and God did not withhold his own Son as proof of that love.

But the exile still threatens. There are more things that may separate us from God, so Paul makes a final statement. This final statement begins with one of the strongest words in Greek: πειθω. This means trust, confidence, rely on, be certain of. If one is certain of something

147

then there is nothing that can undermine that confidence. It is the rock upon which you build your life. The idea against which you judge everything else you do.

"I am convinced, πειθω, that neither death, nor life, nor angels, nor rulers, nor things present, nor things to come, nor powers, nor height, nor depth, nor anything else in all creation, will be able to separate us from the love of God in Christ Jesus our Lord." Nothing in all creation can violently tear us away from the love of God that God demonstrated for us in the life, death, and resurrection of Jesus Christ. Nothing, not political rulers; nor things we cannot imagine yet; not even the tragic, unimaginable death of one so beloved can separate not just me, not just you, but **_us_** from the love of God in Christ Jesus our Lord. ... Hope!

My friends let me ask you to reach out your hand, to grasp the hand of one sitting near you. If you need to move just a bit closer to someone else, that's ok. I will wait a minute.

How can we sing the Lord's song in exile? We sing together. Hold on to one another because we cannot do this alone. We know pain, hurt, tears, and loss. But I am convinced that God is faithful always and

nothing,

    nothing,

        nothing,

            can separate **_us_** from the love of God in Christ Jesus our Lord.

Places of Honor
Mark 10:35-45

Kirkin' o' the Tartans

35 James and John, the sons of Zebedee, came forward to him and said to him, "Teacher, we want you to do for us whatever we ask of you." 36 And he said to them, "What is it you want me to do for you?" 37 And they said to him, "Grant us to sit, one at your right hand and one at your left, in your glory." 38 But Jesus said to them, "You do not know what you are asking. Are you able to drink the cup that I drink, or be baptized with the baptism that I am baptized with?" 39 They replied, "We are able." Then Jesus said to them, "The cup that I drink you will drink; and with the baptism with which I am baptized, you will be baptized; 40 but to sit at my right hand or at my left is not mine to grant, but it is for those for whom it has been prepared."

41 When the ten heard this, they began to be angry with James and John. 42 So Jesus called them and said to them, "You know that among the Gentiles those whom they recognize as their rulers lord it over them, and their great ones are tyrants over them. 43 But it is not so among you; but whoever wishes to become great among you must be your servant, 44 and whoever wishes to be first among you must be slave of all. 45 For the Son of Man came not to be served but to serve, and to give his life a ransom for many."

When I was in high school, this scripture text was one of my favorites. "Whoever wishes to be great among you must be your servant, and whoever wishes to be first among you must be slave of all. For the Son of Man came not to be served but to serve, and to give his life a ransom for many." Yes, a life of service to others. That's what following Jesus is all about right? It absolutely is. But like James and John, and all the other disciples for that matter, when I was in high school I had no clue what that really meant. Today, while I still find it so powerful as an idea, I am still not quite sure what it means in actual practice.

For as Professor Sarah Hinkley Wilson writes:

Oh, James and John, you foolish boys. *Of course*, following Jesus doesn't mean being powerful like the rulers of the Gentiles. *Of course*, it's all about servant leadership. Jesus is so deep, and you're so shallow. Then we good Christians scout out clever ways to "serve" in self-aggrandizing fashion, as immortalized in the words of Weird Al [Yankovic]'s "Amish Paradise": *"You know I'm a million times as humble as thou art."*[92]

Yes, how many of us can truly declare, with real humility, that we live a life not of self-interest, but of service to all? How many of us really model our days on Jesus' life who gave his life as a ransom for many? It is oh so easy for us to point fingers at James and John and their request for places of honor when Jesus comes into his glory, but it would probably be wise for us to ask if we are really doing that much better.

Even today, think about this service of worship. Kirkin' o' the Tartans! It is one of my favorite services of the year with the bagpipes, the drums, and the tartan flags. Liturgy drawn from our Scottish brothers and sisters in faith. A full sanctuary and a lunch to follow! It is glorious, right? But we need to ask ourselves, not just today but every Sunday, is this what Jesus had in mind for his disciples when he said, "Whoever wishes to be great among you must be your servant, and whoever wishes to be first among you must be slave of all. For the Son of Man came not to be served but to serve, and to give his life a ransom for many."

This week as I read those verses again and again, as I reflected upon James and John's request which got the whole episode started, I have been thinking about my own seat here in this magnificent sanctuary on this glorious Sunday. For James and John ask to sit on Jesus' right and left in his glory. Almost every Sunday I sit in that chair right there, on the *right* of the Lord's Table. And it is a pretty nice chair - one of the only seats in this entire sanctuary that has a cushion! I may have mentioned to you before but this is the only church I have served as pastor in which the preacher's chair sits right out in the

---

[92] Sarah Hinkley Wilson, "Commentary on Mark 10:35-45," http://www.workingpreacher.org/preaching.aspx?commentary_id=3799

open, not hidden at all by the pulpit or other chancel furniture. It is a seat designed and placed so that the entire congregation can see the one who sits in it. And I am immensely, immensely grateful for the opportunity and gift it is for me to sit in that chair. But, my friends, I recognize that I sit in a privileged seat much like the one James and John wanted.

So, what do we do when we recognize both the privilege we enjoy and that Jesus calls us to be servants? I know that I have preached sermons before about the importance of serving others. I trust that the fine preachers who preceded me sitting in that chair preached those sermons as well because service is at the heart of the gospel. And I trust that you hear those sermons and believe them just as I believe them when I preach them. And yet, all of us – me very much included – all of us as we leave this magnificent sanctuary return to our lives of privilege largely unmoved. As my friend and the editor of *The Presbyterian Outlook*, Jill Duffield says,

> We want Jesus to do for us what we ask of him - and when was the last time you asked Jesus to make you last of all? When was the last time you asked Jesus to make you a servant? When was the last time you heard a prayer in worship that said something like: "God, take away our status and our power, make us the least and the last." … What might happen if we printed mission statements like that on our bulletins? Maybe, "First Presbyterian Church: Striving to be last." … [or] How about "Least Presbyterian Church"? [93]

Yes, my friends what do we do with our privilege and Jesus' call for us to be servants? I think we begin like I did this morning with a confession that we do not really understand what Jesus is talking about any more than James and John did. But we do have one advantage they did not. We stand on the other side of the cross and the resurrection. We keep asking God for places of honor and seats of glory, and somehow God keeps loving us anyway. We cannot

---

[93] Jill Duffield, "22nd Sunday after Pentecost – October 21, 2018," https://pres-outlook.org/2018/10/22nd-sunday-after-pentecost-october-21-2018/

escape the power of exploitation, privilege, idolatry, and the lure of safety – it is the water we swim in – but that is exactly what God has saved us from in Jesus Christ our Lord. Again, Jill Duffield writes.

> James and John want glory. Jesus offers salvation. James and John want status. Jesus offers relationship. James and John want power. Jesus offers purpose. James and John want greatness. Jesus offers life. James and John want recognition. Jesus offers grace. James and John want vindication. Jesus offers mercy. James and John, like gentiles then and now, want to lord it over others. Jesus offers them, and us, the privilege of serving side by side, with him. We want to be first, but Jesus reminds us that we are closest to him when we are among the least and last and lost.[94]

Yes, my friends, first we confess our privilege and that we do not really understand what it means to be least and last and lost. And then we seek to follow Jesus. That remains the call for all of us – to follow Jesus. And sometimes, like this morning, we follow Jesus with bagpipes, and drums, and tartan flags. But as we celebrate the Kirkin' o' the Tartans we do so not just in remembrance of Saint Columba who brought Christianity to Scotland in the 500s, or the warrior William Wallace of Scottish Independence in 1297 and *Braveheart* movie fame, or fiery John Knox of the Scottish Reformation in 1560.

No, we would do well to lift up David Livingstone, a Scottish physician who traveled as a missionary to Africa in the 1800s and who seemingly had disappeared until found by Henry Stanley who famously said, "Dr. Livingstone, I presume."[95]

We would remember the Scottish Olympic Athlete Eric Liddell who refused to run a race on the Sabbath in the 1924 Olympics but won the gold medal in another event. Instead of basking in his glory and

---

[94] Ibid.
[95] "David Livingstone: Biography," https://www.biography.com/people/david-livingstone-9383955

triumph, Liddell traveled to China as a missionary the next year and eventually died in an internment camp for his faith.[96]

We would celebrate Jain Haining who volunteered for service as a missionary in 1932, becoming the matron of the girls' home at the Scottish Mission School in Budapest, Hungary. Many of her students were Jewish.

When the war broke out, church authorities ordered Ms. Haining to return to Scotland no fewer than three times, but she refused declaring, "I shall continue to do my duty...and stick to my post."

Jain Haining was arrested in April 1944 and detained by the Gestapo, accused of working among Jews. She was sent to Auschwitz and died "in hospital," code for the gas chamber, on July 17 of that year.[97]

Yes, my friends, we celebrate the Kirkin' o' the Tartans and it is a privilege to do so. But the privilege of this service, the privilege of that seat, and the privilege of the pews in which you sit cannot be merely for us. Let us enlist our privilege in service of the voices of those long silenced. Let us weave a new thread into the old tartans because there is always room for another. Let us stand with and beside those in need of peace, and hope, and justice.

I admit, I do not fully understand what that looks like, but let that not be an excuse for inaction. For Christ has called us both to recognize our privilege and to serve. It was Scottish *émigré*, the Reverend Dr. Peter Marshall, who said,

> When a group of people, no matter how small or ordinary, was willing to die out to their selfish desires, the life which

---

[96] "A Short Biography of Eric H. Liddell," https://www.ericliddell.org/about-us/eric-liddell/biography/
[97] Steven Brocklehurst, "Jane Haining: The Scot who Died in Auschwitz," https://www.bbc.com/news/uk-scotland-30119673

came out of that death was immeasurable and continued to affect lives far into the future.[98]

May that be so for you and for me long after the last note of the piper fades.

---

[98] Peter Marshall, *The Light and the Glory*,
https://www.goodreads.com/work/quotes/804217-the-light-and-the-glory

Calling All God's Children Home
Jeremiah 31:7-9

7 For thus says the LORD:
Sing aloud with gladness for Jacob,
  and raise shouts for the chief of the nations;
proclaim, give praise, and say,
  "Save, O LORD, your people,
  the remnant of Israel."
8 See, I am going to bring them from the land of the north,
  and gather them from the farthest parts of the earth,
among them the blind and the lame,
  those with child and those in labor, together;
  a great company, they shall return here.
9 With weeping they shall come,
  and with consolations I will lead them back,
I will let them walk by brooks of water,
  in a straight path in which they shall not stumble;
for I have become a father to Israel,
  and Ephraim is my firstborn.

It was in January of 2006 when I first made the trip to Aberdeen, Scotland to take classes as part of my Doctor of Ministry degree studies. I try to save a dollar when I can, especially on airfare, so I booked the cheapest flight I could find. If you have flown to Europe, you may remember that most flights leave the states in early evening so that, with the time change, you arrive in England or Europe in the morning the next day. That was the case with my flight, so I left Charlotte in the evening and arrived at Heathrow Airport in London about 8 AM London time.

What I had not fully appreciated in my effort to be cheap was that I then had an eight-hour layover in the Heathrow Airport before my flight to Aberdeen. I was already exhausted, so I sat near my gate, essentially by myself, all day long. I had reading to do for my classes, so it was not a total waste of time, but it was a long day. Finally, we boarded the plane for Aberdeen, and I found myself sitting next to a quite drunk Scotsman who believed Christianity was a bunch of rubbish (to clean up his language quite a bit) ... but that is a story for another time.

I arrived in Aberdeen, retrieved my luggage and waited for the person from the college who was supposed to pick me up. I waited and I waited, and I waited. It was about an hour later that I realized my mistake. I had misread the time of my arrival in Aberdeen due to Scotland's use of military or 24-hour time. So, if my ride had come to get me, she had left the airport long ago. I was alone, probably 16 hours after I had left home, in a foreign country, not thinking clearly due to fatigue, not familiar with the customs or how to arrange for my own transportation. It was the most alone and unwelcome I think I have ever felt.

Have you ever felt like that before? Maybe it was a time that you took a wrong turn on a trip and became utterly lost. Maybe it was when you sat for the first time in a new class in a new school and didn't know a soul. Maybe it was when your mom or your dad or your husband or your wife walked out the door carrying a suitcase and never came back. Maybe it was when you sat in an exam room wondering when the doctor would come back with your test results. Maybe it was when you stood, because you couldn't sit any longer, in a hospital waiting room while someone you loved underwent surgery. Maybe it was when you walked into your house three days after the funeral of your spouse, your family and friends had gone home, and you realized there was no one there to greet you. Yes, I suspect we have all felt alone.

My friend and mentor Tom Currie recently suggested that in addition to these situational occasions, there is another form of loneliness that characterizes life today. He says that it "resembles a lostness, an aimlessness, disconnected and unrelated to others ... a quiet despair that pervades our conversations and manners ... we come not to expect much [of life]."[99]

Perhaps you know that kind of loneliness as well. Maybe you are busy all day with the children, but long for even one word of adult

---

[99] Thomas W. Currie, "With Head Held High: Preaching Hope in a Noisy Time," *Journal for Preachers, Vol. XLII, No 1,* 4.

conversation. Perhaps you check Facebook a hundred times a day hoping to see something to make you smile but end up feeling more alone despite your thousands of "friends." Maybe your children are teenagers and they don't talk to you much anymore. You don't seem to get together with other parents anymore either. Or maybe you are the teenager and you know the other side of that story - everyone else at school seems happy, but you're not. Bullies used to have to insult you to your face. Now texts and posts flood your account 24 hours a day. You can't tell mom and dad because they are so busy, and they won't understand.

Yes, I think we can all recognize the loneliness that is pervasive in our world today. But before we dwell there too long, I want to proclaim some good news to you this morning. Yes, we need to hear some good news.

And here it is - God welcomes you. Let me say it again - You are welcomed and embraced and loved by a God who will never leave you alone. Emmanuel, God with us - that is who our God is. You and I are never completely alone. We may feel alone and abandoned and uncared for and unloved, but we are not. No matter what you have done, where you have been, or what you have experienced God welcomes you and loves you. Yes, we are always in the presence and warmth and strength and love and care of God who has stretched out his arms on a cross to embrace you and me. We are not alone. By God's grace we belong to a God who loves us - warts and sins and all.

And the church, the people of God, is one place where we should know and experience that welcome, that sense of belonging, that sense that we are not alone. The church should be a place where we meet and encounters our risen Lord. This is big stuff; most important stuff. Yes, here in the church is a place where we can come to know Christ in a real and even an intimate way. It is a place to know Christ's love and care and compassion. The church is the place where you and I can know the same kind of joy that I felt when I finally saw a Doctor of Ministry classmate walk into that airport in Aberdeen. I trust that you have felt that here in this church and it is why you have come back again and again. If today is your first day with us, I pray you find Christ's love and compassion and welcome here so that you too will want to come back again and again.

My friends, I want you to hear, really hear and know this good news – God loves you and the church is a place where you can know and experience God's love. You are not alone.

That is what this scripture text from Jeremiah is all about. The people of Israel have been in exile in Babylon. They are far from home. They felt abandoned and alone. But, finally, through the prophet God declares:

> [7] Sing aloud with gladness for Jacob,
>   and raise shouts for the chief of the nations;
> proclaim, give praise, and say,
>   "Save, O LORD, your people,
>   the remnant of Israel."
> [8] See, I am going to bring them from the land of the north,
>   and gather them from the farthest parts of the earth,
> among them the blind and the lame,
>   those with child and those in labor, together;
>   a great company, they shall return here.
> [9] With weeping they shall come,
>   and with consolations I will lead them back,
> I will let them walk by brooks of water,
>   in a straight path in which they shall not stumble;
> for I have become a father to Israel,
>   and Ephraim is my firstborn.

Yes, God declares that he is going to bring all the children home. Not because they are strong enough or smart enough or accomplished enough. Not because they have finally figured out life or have left their struggles behind. No, from the farthest parts of the earth, God will gather the blind and the lame, those carrying a child and those in labor, those weeping and those who stumble. God is calling all the children home.

My friends, that is the call that God is offering you today. From the youngest infant to our oldest saints; from the frazzled parent of a toddler to the bewildered parent of teen; from the youth bombarded by social media to the senior who is wary of the internet; from the travelers far from home to the grieved and the lost; from the new residents to those who have lived here all their life; from those who worship here often to those who entered this sanctuary for the first time today; God is calling you, God is calling me, God is calling all the children home.

My friends, come home. There is a place for you. You are loved and welcome here. You need not be alone.

CPSIA information can be obtained
at www.ICGtesting.com
Printed in the USA
FSHW022358250519
58399FS

9 781949 888546